The Cheapskate's Guide to
BRANSON, MISSOURI

The Cheapskate's Guide to
BRANSON, MISSOURI

Hotels, Entertainment, Restaurants,
Recreation, Special Events, and More

CONNIE EMERSON

CITADEL PRESS
Kensington Publishing Group
www.kensingtonbooks.com

CITADEL PRESS BOOKS are published by

Kensington Publishing Corp.
850 Third Avenue
New York, NY 10022

All Kensington titles, imprints, and distributed lines are available at special quantity discounts for bulk purchases for sales promotions, premiums, fund-raising, educational, or institutional use. Special book excerpts or customized printings can also be created to fit specific needs. For details, write or phone the office of the Kensington special sales manager: Kensington Publishing Corp., 850 Third Avenue, New York, NY 10022, attn: Special Sales Department, phone 1-800-221-2647.

Citadel Press and the Citadel Logo are trademarks of Kensington Publishing Corp.

First printing: March 2002

10   9   8   7   6   5   4   3   2   1

Printed in the United States of America

Library of Congress Control Number: TK

ISBN 0-0865-2284-4

Contents

Branson has been around for a while, but only in the past ten years has it attracted a lot of attention. Now it ranks eighteenth among America's favorite vacation places. And as people who have been there know, it may well rank number one as a bargain spot.

To start out on the right travel foot, saving money as you go, requires advance planning. Whether it's finding the lowest airfare, booking the best accommodations in your price range, or minimizing phone charges once you're on your way, we tell you how to do it.

With hundreds of hotels, motels and other lodging places in Branson, it's not hard to find a place to lay your head. What's difficult is to get the ultimate in satisfaction for the money you spend.

Although Branson restaurants usually serve up tasty meals, the majority of the 350 eating places in town are pretty much alike. You'll get our take on the best of the buffets and our favorite restaurants with menus. We've included ideas for a week's worth of picnics, too.

Acknowledgments

When I began writing the Cheapskate's series of guidebooks, I pondered the seeming impossibility of finding out *everything* about a place. How could anyone discover the best places to eat, to shop, to sleep—not to mention how to save money? In the following weeks it became apparent that all a writer needs is a lot of curiosity, a little bit of help from her friends, and a lot of advice, information, and help from people she has never met before.

My friends and informants who helped enormously in putting this book together date back to 1988, when I first visited Branson. It was a sleepy little town in those days; Bill Jones was head of the chamber of commerce and Margaret Eiche took me around to show me the sights. Their help and hospitality was matched by the 2001 staff at the Branson Chamber of Commerce, especially Mandy Schwarz, a whiz at making arrangements.

I want to acknowledge, too, the input of my colleagues in the Society of American Travel Writers and of my dear friend Dorothy West, whose tour group experiences gave me insights I otherwise would not have had. Much of the material for this book came from people whose names I will never know—the couple who steered me to a scenic overlook, overheard conversations that led me to explore this shop and that restaurant, the preteen boys who filled me in on Branson's arcade scene. Though they will always remain anonymous, their advice—consciously or unwittingly given—is greatly appreciated.

Thanks, also, to the staff at Kensington Books—especially to Bruce Bender for suggesting the idea and Ann LaFarge for editing. And last, but by no means least, a big thank-you to Ralph, whose domestic tranquility is destroyed whenever book deadlines approach.

Introduction

Crazy about country music? Like lakes, rolling hills, and a laid-back lifestyle?

Want to get away for a few days without spending a small fortune? Your answer may be Branson, Missouri—sometimes called the Country Music Capital of the United States and Live Entertainment Capital of the World.

Snuggled in the Ozarks on the shores of Lake Taneycomo and Table Rock Lake, Branson is just forty miles south of Springfield, Missouri, and eleven miles north of the Arkansas state line. Although excavated artifacts indicate that bluff dwellers lived in the area about three thousand years ago, Branson was still a sleepy little village in 1896 when an ailing minister-turned-novelist named Howard Bell Wright traveled to the Ozarks in hopes of getting well. Shortly after arriving from his home in the East, Wright had stopped near Branson at the Mutton Hollow homestead of John and Anna Ross when the flood-swollen White River forced him to abandon his plans to ride on horseback into the rugged hills.

He had planned to spend only one night, the story goes, but ended up staying with the Ross family for the entire summer, returning each of the following eight summers as he slowly regained his health. During one of these summers—1902—drought pushed the homesteaders to near-starvation as crops shriveled, streams dried up, and wild game disappeared. The settlers' desperation led to a series of events around which Wright built the plot of a novel called *Shepherd of the Hills*.

Published in 1907, his book sold more than one million copies when it first came out, and kept on selling as years went by. As a result, the book's fans began flocking to Branson to see the story's setting and the hillbillies Wright described in it.

Many of the first-time tourists became repeat visitors and told their friends about the area. They found that the White River—and the lakes formed when dams were built across it— were great for fishing and water sports. The weather was pleasant almost year-round, and there were caves and other natural attractions to explore.

As the tourist count increased, musical performances showcasing regional talent were presented at venues near the caves. Artisans sold their wares from their studios, front porches, or local gift shops. When in 1959 the four Mabes brothers set up folding chairs in the community hall at Branson and put on their twice-weekly Baldknobbers Jubilee, the area began its metamorphosis from a recreation spot to a live music performance center. In 2000, Branson attracted well over seven million visitors.

The numbers keep climbing each year, so that now Branson attracts more tourists than such long-established destinations as Colonial Williamsburg and Nashville. The number of attractions and activities has steadily increased. Whereas there were only twenty-two theaters in 1988, there are now forty—presenting a total of about eighty shows daily.

Even if you don't give a hoot and a holler about country music, you won't be bored. Silver Dollar City (see chapter 11, Day Trips) is one of the most interesting theme parks in the country—one that adults enjoy even more than children. Since area lakes, unlike those formed by glaciers in the northern part of the United States, came about as a result of reclamation project dams being built on the rivers, they're irregularly shaped, with lots of squiggles and miles of shoreline to explore. Hiking trails meander through the hills.

The abundance of lakeshore lots, coupled with the region's natural beauty, has resulted in a sizable retirement community. Too, the area's economic potential and natural beauty have helped convince big-name entertainers, tired of always being on the road, that settling down in Branson would be a grand idea.

As it has grown, the town—due to the roller-coaster terrain—hasn't been able to spread out in grid fashion like most population centers. Instead, there are great open spaces that remain undeveloped, with long rows of restaurants, theaters, and other businesses lining the more buildable ridges. The new subdivisions have been built on plateaus above the lakes, with the city limits covering more than seventeen square miles.

One of the ridges—the town's main artery along Missouri Highway 76—stretches for about five miles. Other ridges are crowned with Shepherd of the Hills Expressway, Green Mountain Drive, Gretna and Roark Valley Roads, each of which passes by an ever-increasing number of shopping centers, theaters, and motor hotels.

Branson homes range from modest frame dwellings built in the 1920s and earlier to multimillion-dollar lakefront estates. There are churches in abundance—nine of them Baptist, the most common religious affiliation of the town's residents. Schools, parks, and public buildings look much like those anywhere else. In fact, without its entertainment areas, Branson could be Everytown, Middle America.

As popular a destination as Branson has become, it doesn't appeal to everyone. It's definitely not for young singles and couples who like trendy shops, restaurants, and nightspots (the average visitor age is 55.9 years old). Travelers whose vacation enjoyment is enhanced by gourmet meals and deluxe accommodations, sophisticated shows and upscale shopping should probably choose other destinations. Driving can be difficult, because of both the traffic and the hills, which can become especially treacherous in winter. People who hate standing in lines and are uncomfortable in crowds will find the summer vacation period difficult and should consider visiting Branson in the off season.

Then, too, there's a certain religious and nationalistic thread that weaves through much of the entertainment and might not be in sync with everybody's life philosophy. Many of the shows have a conservative Christian orientation (some of the performers even give testimonials on stage), and there's a good deal of patriotic fervor as well. There are commercial tour companies, in fact, that specialize in arranging Branson trips for church groups (see chapter 2, Branson Bedtime)

For adults and families who are seeking "totally suitable"

entertainment and are anxious to get full value for money spent, however, Branson can be a winner. It's a natural, too, for people who love outdoor activities, and to whom sophisticated entertainment and amenities are secondary.

This book is divided into twelve chapters, each of them exploring a component—such as accommodations, dining, attractions, activities, excursions, and shopping—that can enhance or detract from a Branson holiday. Since vacation budgets vary as much as travelers' attitudes and interests do, we have researched both luxury and economy lodgings; free entertainment and expensive treats; discount outlets and stores that handle one-of-a-kind handcrafts—as well as goods and services in the midprice range.

Read the parts of the book that fit your vacation profile; skip those that don't. Always remember that there are no universally "right" and "wrong" ways to travel. So forget about what your friends, relatives, and neighbors say you ought to do (unless you want to). After all, only the travel styles that fit your own needs and preferences are right for you.

THE CHEAPSKATE'S GUIDE TO
BRANSON, MISSOURI

1

Making Plans

PUTTING IT TOGETHER

Branson is one of the best vacation spots in the country for bargains. Whether you're on a bare-bones budget or looking for low-cost luxury, you'll find that discounts are available for just about everything you need to make your holiday special.

The more lead time you have, the more information you'll get—information that translates into value for the money you spend, whether it's for transportation, accommodations, food, or sight-seeing. You'll be able to find deals almost everywhere when you go shopping. So start making plans as soon as you decide on a Branson holiday.

The first thing you need to do is collect all the information you can lay your hands on (see chapter 12, For More Information). You'll want to read up on accommodations, because that's where the biggest savings can be made. Obtain as many hotel and motel brochures and rate sheets as you can. Even though we all know that the room, garden, and pool area pictures in the brochures have been photographed from their most flattering angles, pictures are still our best way of determining what the hotels and motels look like. Transportation costs take a big chunk out of vacation budgets, too, so do the research necessary to find out which mode is best for you. As far as attractions and shows are concerned, the more you know about them in advance, the better the chance you'll have of seeing the shows you like as well as saving entertainment dollars.

To help ensure a happy time for all, it's also a good idea to define your expectations. Whether you're going alone, as a couple, as a family with children, or with a group of friends, it's important to find out what activities each person is interested in, as well as the kind of accommodations and meals preferred. If you're not traveling alone, it's also a good idea to determine whether the people in your group want to go as a group to meals, shows, shopping, and sight-seeing during the entire trip or if you should build free time into your itinerary for individual excursions. Pretrip discussion is especially important when some people in the group want to be on the go from morning to night, while others prefer a more relaxed pace. Most differences in interests and tastes among people traveling as a group can be accommodated when solutions have been worked out in advance.

Since the Branson entertainment emphasis is on shows, most visitors take in several performances—the average is four—while they're in town. If attending shows is of paramount importance to you, you'll want to know what's playing. In fact, the dates you decide on for your visit may be influenced by the fact that certain shows are scheduled for that time. And after you've made your show choices, in order to avoid disappointment, it's a good idea to reserve tickets in advance, especially during June and July when the most popular shows can be sellouts.

For visitors whose primary vacation recreation revolves around fishing or golf or theme parks, other considerations such as the season, crowds, and weather will come into play. While there are people who attend three or even four shows a day or fish from dawn to dusk, most area visitors prefer a combination of shows, sight-seeing, shopping, and outdoor activities.

Whatever their leisure time choices, almost all tourists who aren't on tours will need to make decisions about what transportation to take and where to stay. If you have a good travel agent, enlist his or her services. Get quotes on round-trip airfare, information and prices for accommodations, and brochures about organized tours, as well as recommendations. Be advised, however, that while travel agents in some parts of North America have large numbers of Branson-bound clients, others have had few occasions to make Branson bookings. In general, you'll find agents who are most knowledgeable about Branson in places like Chicago, Dallas, Kansas City, Little Rock, Memphis, Milwaukee, Oklahoma City, and St. Louis.

Bargain Trip?

Half the country's population lives within a day's drive of Branson. No wonder, then, that the bulk of its tourists come from that part of the country. It is such an important target area for time-share companies that some people don't even have to pay for their Branson trips. Time-share salespeople telephone preselected couples throughout Middle America, offering trips to Branson that are free or available at incredibly low prices. The catch is that people who accept the offer have to spend a lot of their time looking at promotional videos and listening to sales pitches. In addition, the salespeople are so convincing that a significant proportion of the people who come for the bargain trip end up buying a time-share for thousands of dollars.

If you have the time, you might decide to do your own research. In some areas, you'll have to spend a significant amount of effort searching for brochures; in others, they'll be in display racks at every travel agency and advertised in every newspaper's travel section.

People who are at ease with the Internet can use search engines such as **Yahoo, Google, AltaVista,** and **Ask Jeeves** to get information on airlines, hotels, and motels, as well as various tour companies' itineraries, amenities, and prices (chapter 12, For More Information, contains a list of useful Web sites).

After you've investigated your options, you can either have a travel agent make the arrangements or make your own reservations by phone or Internet. I have found that the most satisfactory way to plan my travels is by doing a lot of the research myself before consulting an agent. Together we decide whether having the agent make the reservations or doing it myself will be most advantageous as far as both of us are concerned. Sometimes Internet deals beat any a travel agent can find; at other times, packages are available to agents that aren't sold directly to the general public. Travel agents also on occasion get flyers or e-mail announcements of promotions that are real winners as far as value is concerned.

Branson Visitor Profile
- 83 percent of Branson visitors travel to Branson by personal vehicle
- 31 percent come as part of family groups
- 69 percent of visitors are seniors (average age is 55.9 years)
- Average length of stay is 3.9 nights

EXAMINING YOUR OPTIONS

Without question, the fastest and most expensive way to travel from any distance to Branson (population 6,000) is by air. Private plane pilots fly in to **M. Graham Clark Airport** at College of the Ozarks, one mile from Branson, while commercial and charter planes land at, and depart from, the **Springfield/Branson Regional Airport**, about forty miles away. Among the commercial airlines with scheduled flights to Springfield/Branson are:

American Eagle Airlines	800/433-7300
Northwest Airlink	800/225-2525
United Express Airlines	800/241-6522
US Airways Express	800/428-4322

What isn't so obvious is that while airfare to Springfield/Branson is pricey, there are bargains to be had. Whatever airline you choose, in order to pay the least and get the best, you have to either plan early, be very lucky, or be able to travel on a few days' notice. Shop around for the best deals by checking out the ads in newspaper travel sections and in publications like *Consumer Reports Travel Letter*. Check out each of the airline's Web sites as well as discount travel Web sites such as www.Orbitz.com and www.bestfares.com to find the lowest fares.

When you're flexible and willing to tolerate a bit of inconvenience, you have a good chance to save money. You can cut transportation costs by flying on the days of the week when passenger loads are traditionally the lightest (usually Saturday, Tuesday, Wednesday, and Thursday). Red-eye flights often cost less than those scheduled for more convenient hours.

The time of year figures into the cost equation as well. However, since airfares are generally lowest in the winter months, it's necessary to balance the savings against factors such as cold weather, crowds during the holiday special events, and fewer shows offered during slow periods.

There are cases, of course, where only one airline serves your point of departure. If fares are exorbitant—and they frequently are in monopoly situations—explore other options. A larger airport where airlines compete for business may be a two-hour drive farther, or a three-hour bus ride away. Most of us don't mind that kind of inconvenience if it will save us a couple of hundred dollars on each ticket. For example, people who live in the eastern Dakotas and western Minnesota often drive to Minneapolis instead of using the smaller airports that are closer to home, since much better deals are available at this Northwest Airlines hub. Residents who live in Milwaukee may find that driving to Chicago's O'Hare will save them money. And people who live in densely populated areas on the East Coast more often than not have several airport choices.

For example, in September 2001 the lowest round-trip fare from Minneapolis to Springfield/Branson advertised on a Web site was $249.48, by United. Total flight time was about four hours. Northwest's price was almost identical, at $250. With a connection in Memphis, the trip took about four hours and fifteen minutes.

From Fargo, North Dakota, a four-hour drive from the Minneapolis–St. Paul airport, the flight to Springfield on United took six and a half hours and cost $330.62, while the

Northwest flight cost $350. Two people traveling together could save $160 (minus the cost of gas and parking fees) by flying from Minneapolis on Northwest, but only about $89 by driving to Sioux Falls, South Dakota, or Minneapolis and taking the United flight from there.

United's lowest-price flight from Denver to Springfield/ Branson during the same period was $310.04, while the flight from Cheyenne, Wyoming—about a two-hour drive away— was a whopping $490.02. A couple could save $360 (minus gas and long-term parking fees) by making the two-hour trip to Denver by car and catching the plane there.

These fares may at times be even lower when sold by an Internet discounter. The Minneapolis–Springfield fare listed above was $10 less as advertised on www.Orbitz.com.

When a low fare is advertised in the newspaper, fast action is required to get in on the deal, because the number of tickets is limited. But don't despair if only the most expensive tickets are available from the airline for your travel dates. Although their reservations people may have sold out all the cheap tickets alloted to the flights you want, discounted tickets may be available from other sources. Every unsold seat on a flight means money that can never be recaptured, and people watching the airlines' bottom lines don't want that to happen. Therefore, when they anticipate light loads on specific routes, they sell blocks of tickets at drastically reduced prices to wholesalers, who sell their unsold inventory to discounters.

Airlines also sell surplus tickets to travel agencies that specialize in discounting. These so-called bucket shops used to have a shady reputation, but have now established themselves as reliable businesses. They are listed in the yellow pages of telephone directories and do most of their advertising via the newspapers.

More often than not, discounted tickets have no advance purchase requirement. They're usually nonrefundable and can be used only on the issuing airline. This means that when a flight is canceled, you're grounded until there's space on one of that airline's subsequent flights. Before you advance any money, check with the Better Business Bureau if you have any doubts regarding the discounter.

Among the larger, well-established operators offering discounted Branson tickets and tours are:

Encore/Short Notice
4501 Forbes Boulevard
Lanham, MD 20706
301/459-8020
(membership fee)

Last Minute Travel
1249 Boylston Street
Boston, MA 02215
800/527-8646

Traveler's Advantage
3033 South Parker Road, Suite 1000
Aurora, CO 80014
800/548-1116
(membership fee)

Travel sections in major North American newspapers almost always contain advertisements of ticket brokers in their respective areas.

A number of charter airlines also fly to Springfield/Branson Regional Airport, in addition to regularly scheduled commercial flights. To find out about flights that originate in your part of the country, contact your local travel agent.

When you have a choice between a charter flight and a discounted ticket on an airline with regular service, choose the latter—even if the ticket is somewhat more expensive. When a regular airline flight is canceled, passengers are put on the airline's next available flight or ticketed on another airline that flies the same route. Charters usually don't have more than one flight a day to a particular destination, so if the flight is canceled, you probably won't be flying that day.

Since many airline passengers want to rent cars when they arrive, you'll find that most of the well-known firms, as well as some locals, have agencies at the airport (see chapter 4, Getting Around).

COMMERCIAL TOURS

You won't have to budget time for making transportation and accommodation arrangements if you decide to take a package tour, but you will need to make decisions as to which tour will satisfy you the most. Your choices should depend on your interests and physical ability as well as price. There are choices galore, since dozens of tour companies throughout North America provide tours to Branson, and an extraordinary number of companies based in Branson offer tours as well.

If you decide on a commercial tour, you have the choice of taking one that originates near your hometown or providing your own transportation to Branson (or the Springfield/Branson Regional Airport) and joining the tour upon arrival. The majority of Branson visitors come from nearby states— Arkansas, Illinois, Indiana, Iowa, Kansas, Minnesota, Missouri, Tennessee, Texas, and Wisconsin—so tours leave from various points within those states, many of them on a regular basis. You can find out about these tours by contacting your local travel agency and by reading the ads in the travel sections of area newspapers.

Although there aren't as many in some regions as in others, you'll also find tours originating in almost all parts of North America. For example, in 2001 Deluxe Tours, based in Toronto, offered a nine-day motorcoach tour that involved two and a half days of travel each way and a four-night stay in Branson. Included in the price—$1,195 Canadian for a couple; $1,675 Canadian for single occupancy—were eight continental breakfasts, four shows, transportation to Silver Dollar City and Ride the Ducks, plus an Amish dinner en route. Accommodations in Branson were at the Hampton Inn.

Tour Link of Palm Harbor, Florida's, nine-day tour in 2001 ($599 per person double occupancy) included motorcoach transportation, eight nights' lodging (the Colonnade Hotel in Branson), seven shows, and fourteen meals.

United Airlines Travel Options 2001 tours to Branson included round-trip airfare from any United Airlines city in Arizona, California, Idaho, Nevada, New Mexico, Oregon,

Washington, or Utah; five nights at a three-star hotel; five breakfasts, two lunches, and two dinners; and the Shoji Tabuchi, Bobby Vinton, *Showboat Branson Belle,* Platters, Yakov Smirnoff, and Buck Trent Breakfast shows, plus an excursion to Silver Dollar City. Price per person, double occupancy, was $1,128 plus air taxes. Single supplement was $196, and the land-only portion of the tour cost $788.

An equally large number of tours and packages are offered to people who travel to Branson on their own. Some of these packages are put together by tour operators and others by individual hotels and motels (see chapter 2, Branson Bedtime).

Branson Vacation Company offered packages in 2001 ranging from a two-night stay in standard-class lodgings at Edgewood Motel and Reunion Center, one show, continental breakfasts, plus taxes at $122.99 per couple to a five-night package for $599.99 per couple (luxury accommodations at Grand Oaks Hotel, five shows, continental breakfasts, taxes). Fox Tours' two-night packages of lodging, continental breakfasts, and two shows cost from $250 to $275 for two people sharing a room. Prepackaged lodging and entertainment deals either include specific productions or allow the customer to choose from a selected list of shows.

In addition, almost all tour operators and packagers will put together customized tours and packages—arranging accommodations at hotels or lodging places, booking show tickets, supplying cars and drivers for excursions, and adding other features requested by their clients.

Among the companies that offer customized tours for individuals and have been in business for a good while are:

Ozarks' Kirkwood Tour & Travel
P.O. Box 1166
Branson, MO 65615
800/848-5432 or 417/335-4668

Flemming Tours, Inc.
Ozark Mountain Tour Division
P.O. Box 1061
Branson, MO 65615
800/346-7706 or 417/338-6688

Great Southern Travel
1729 West Highway 76
Branson, MO 65616
800/725-7111 or 417/334-8069

Branson tours fall into the following basic categories:

• *Complete Packages.* You will see these tours advertised in
newspaper travel pages and brochures in travel agency racks.
Arrangements for them are finalized months in advance by
the wholesalers that produce them. Occasionally, substitute
lodgings of equal quality are used, but generally the places
where you stay, the shows and attractions that you visit, and
the restaurants where you eat will be those advertised. Some
tour add-ons such as excursions to the little Victorian city of
Eureka, Arkansas, may be optional and require additional
money. All passengers on these tours need to do is make their
reservations, pay their money, pack their bags and be on the
plane or bus when it leaves. These tours may also offer the
best prices, because the wholesaler rents the blocks of rooms,
buys show and attraction tickets, and reserves restaurant table
space in large lots.
• *The Complete Package With Choices.* Offering a variety
of lodging places, restaurants, attractions, and shows, these
packages may also provide discount travel as an option.
Ground transportation is frequently, but not always, the responsibility of the customer.
• *Transportation and Accommodations.* These packages
are generally put together by hotels or motels in conjunction
with an airline that serves the area. They often are the best
bet for independent travelers who want to arrange their own
transportation and itineraries.
• *Transportation, Accommodations, and Meals.* Hotels advertise this kind of package, often with a selection of shows
and/or attractions added (see chapter 2, Branson Bedtime).
• *Customized Tours for Individuals.* You decide what you
want to do, where you want to stay, and the shows and attractions you want to see based on the information or choices the
travel agent or tour operator provides. The agent or tour oper-

ator then makes all the arrangements. This can work out very well if the person guiding your choices is knowledgeable about Branson and concerned solely with quality of product rather than size of commissions.

• *Customized Packages for Groups.* Branson is a popular destination for church groups, family reunions, and members of various organizations. Most tour companies based in Branson offer customized tours that take into account such groups' persuasions and preferences. For instance, Trinity Tours caters to religious groups, highlighting shows based on the life of Christ such as *The Promise* and *Two From Galilee,* as well as productions with a gospel orientation. Restaurants, accommodations, shows, activities, and attractions suitable for three or four generations are integrated into family reunion tour plans.

If you decide that a tour is the best way for you to travel, it's imperative that you find one that is in sync with your travel style. A longtime friend of mine loved Branson, but the pace of the motorcoach tour she took left her exhausted. During a five-night tour, which cost less than $600 per person (double occupancy), she traveled some two thousand miles, stayed at Hampton Inns every night, saw seven shows, visited Silver Dollar City and other area attractions, and went on shopping expeditions. After continental breakfast was served each day at the hotel, tour participants traveled by bus from one event to the next, including meals, and didn't return to their lodgings until after the evening shows.

To avoid being overwhelmed or understimulated, talk to friends who have visited Branson. You'll often get additional information from friends of friends as well. If you can't find anyone who has visited Branson, ask your travel agent for names of people in your area who have taken tours (in some cases, the agent will contact these people for permission before giving you their phone numbers, so the process may take a few days).

When you talk to these people, try to get specific answers about the tours. What did they like best? What didn't they like? Why? Would they use the same tour operator again?

If you take a tour or travel by chartered plane, it's always a good plan to pay by credit card. In the unlikely event that a company goes out of business after you've paid your money but before the trip is over, the people who have the best chance of recovering their money are those who have booked through established travel agencies and paid by credit card.

CAR TALK

Because half of the people in the United States live no more than a day's drive from Branson, it's not surprising that most visitors arrive by car, recreational vehicle, or tour bus (Branson has been voted the number one motorcoach destination every year from 1995 through 2000 by the American Bus Association).

Travel by car, RV, or other private conveyance is the least expensive mode of vacation transportation, especially for two or more people traveling together, even taking into account depreciation on the vehicle and the cost of gasoline. Making sure the vehicle is in excellent running condition before you leave will go a long way toward insuring against unforseen automotive expenses while you're on the road. Items like functional windshield wiper blades, good brakes, and tires with lots of wear left on them are essential for safety.

Visitors who plan to travel to Branson by automobile can log on to the city's Travel & Recreation Information Program (TRIP) at www.branson.tripusa.com for maps showing up-to-the-minute traffic and construction delays and well as weather reports for the Tri-Lakes area. There's also a phone-in information line (417/336-0439 or 877/4TRIP-INFO) for traffic information.

You'll save a lot of time if you buy a good map of Branson in advance of your trip and study it from time to time. These maps are available at bookstores such as Barnes & Noble and on Internet Web sites such as www.amazon.com. The Rand McNally map ($5.95) is a good one, showing the locations of theaters, restaurants, attractions, golf courses, shopping centers, nightspots, and other points of interest.

MILEAGE

Place	Miles	Place	Miles
Alabama:		Missouri:	
Birmingham	488	Kansas City	211
Mobile	644	St. Louis	251
Montgomery	578	Mississippi:	
Arizona:		Biloxi	595
Phoenix	1,321	Jackson	429
Arkansas:		Nebraska:	
Fort Smith	173	Lincoln	409
Little Rock	167	Omaha	401
California:		Nevada:	
Los Angeles	1,652	Las Vegas	1,430
San Francisco	1,948	New Mexico:	
Colorado:		Albuquerque	860
Denver	831	New York:	
District of Columbia:		New York	1,190
Washington, D.C.	1,064	North Carolina:	
Florida		Charlotte	823
Fort Lauderdale	1,274	Ohio:	
Miami	1,291	Cincinnati	596
Orlando	1,071	Cleveland	811
Georgia:		Columbus	669
Atlanta	632	Oklahoma:	
Illinois:		Oklahoma City	321
Chicago	546	Tulsa	219
Indiana:		Pennsylvania:	
Indianapolis	502	Philadelphia	1,125
Iowa:		Pittsburgh	850
Des Moines	395	South Dakota:	
Dubuque	583	Rapid City	917
Sioux City	492	Sioux Falls	578
Kansas:		Tennessee:	
Salina	379	Chattanooga	561
Wichita	303	Memphis	253
Kentucky:		Nashville	432
Lexington	582	Texas:	
Louisville	507	Dallas	415
Louisiana:		Houston	600
New Orleans	585	San Antonio	699
Shreveport	358	Utah:	
Maryland:		Salt Lake City	1,279
Baltimore	1,068	Washington:	
Massachusetts:		Seattle	2,080
Boston	1,414	Wisconsin:	
Michigan:		Green Bay	741
Grand Rapids	693	Madison	611
Detroit	794	Milwaukee	629
Minnesota:			
Duluth	797		
Minneapolis	638		

SUPER SAVERS

Branson visitors who save the most money are usually those who are most flexible—not only as far as their dates of travel are concerned, but also about where they stay and what shows and attractions they see. Savvy travelers may make reservations for their first night in town, but immediately upon arrival start checking out current bargains and taking advantage of every opportunity they find. They head for the Chamber of Commerce Welcome Center and the best assortment of free entertainment publications, brochures, and other sources of money-saving coupons. In addition, they're on the lookout for coupon brochures and free entertainment guides wherever they go—in hotel lobbies, at supermarket entrances, near restaurant waiting areas, in rental car offices, and at convenience stores. Among the free entertainment publications that contain coupons are *TravelHost*, *Sunny Day Guide*, and *Best Read Guide*. *Take 1*, included in the Friday issue of the local newspaper, the *Branson News*, contains coupons you can't find anywhere else.

Savvy travelers are conscious of specials advertised on signs at various business places and one-time offers that may be publicized on radio, TV, and flyers. One of these special offers, in effect from May 15 through September 15, 2001, was called the Gas Busters Rebate. To take advantage of it, visitors had to go to the Chamber of Commerce Welcome Center and show a gas receipt dated within two days of the date presented, along with a valid driver's license. In return they received punch cards worth up to $40 in instant rebates. These rebates were redeemable when the card holder purchased tickets at area shows and attractions or checked in at one of the twenty participating hotels and motels.

Other special offers are valid for several months or even years. Among them are various entertainment packages that pair up two, three, or four shows or attractions. For example, since Silver Dollar City, *Showboat Branson Belle*, Dixie Stampede, and the aquatic amusement park called White Water are all owned by the same corporation, it's only natural that they offer a variety of money-saving show/attraction combinations.

Savings for these packages amount to about 13 to 16 percent, depending on the combination.

Of course, any entertainment package has value only if you want to see the specific shows and attractions that are included. If you're lukewarm about the combination, check to see if discount coupons for the individual segments of the package (or family tickets for the attractions) are available.

Some packages are even "nonbargains." Pricing the components of three different accommodations/show packages advertised by one company in a semiannual entertainment guide, I found that they cost more than if their individual parts had been purchased separately. The several lodging places among the choices had rack rates of about $60 double occupancy during high season (some of them cost as little as $40 per night double occupancy during slow times of the year). Shows were divided into groups A, B, and C.

Two-night/three-show packages, which included one show in each of the A, B, and C categories, cost about $18 more per person than when the lodging and shows were purchased separately. The three-night/four-show (one A, two B, and one C) cost $24 more when sold as a package. The four-night/five-show (two A, two B, and one C) cost $29 more when packaged. Since prices were based on double occupancy, a couple traveling together during high season—and choosing the most expensive shows in each category—would save $36, $48, or $58 total by purchasing the components directly. And that's not taking discount coupons into consideration!

TRIP TIMING

Just a few years ago, if you wanted to see Branson shows, you had to be there between May and October. Now most of the theaters have extended their seasons from mid-April through December, when many theaters present special holiday shows. In an effort to make the area a year-round destination, special events have also been inaugurated that take place during the holidays, January, February, and March. If you dislike the cold or haven't dressed warmly enough, however, you'll wish you had planned your trip for sometime between April and October. The table below gives you each month average high and low temperature. Degrees are Fahrenheit.

Month	High	Low	Precipitation
January	41–43	20–21	1.79″
February	43–51	22–29	2.17″
March	43–51	29–39	2.89″
April	63–72	40–48	4.18″
May	72–80	49–58	4.38″
June	81–88	58–65	5.09″
July	88–91	65–67	2.92″
August	85–98	62–67	3.51″
September	76–85	52–62	4.62″
October	64–75	41–52	3.58″
November	50–63	30–40	3.75″
December	42–50	42–50	3.19″

In addition to rain, precipitation figures include snow, which amounts to a yearly average of twelve inches. What temperature/precipitation charts don't reveal is average heat index, which can make a huge difference in places like Branson. Factoring humidity into the temperature the heat index is more important to your well-being than what the thermometer reads. When the temperature climbs into the nineties and humidity is above 90 percent, it's important to stay as cool as possible, drink lots of liquids, and avoid overexertion.

You'll encounter the biggest crowds during the April to October season, except for the last two weeks in August when the volume of tourists decreases temporarily. Any time of year, however, there are fewer people in town from Monday through Thursday than there are on weekends.

MONEY MANAGEMENT

Planning in advance how much money and time you can spend on your vacation will go a long way toward maintaining your financial health throughout the trip and after you arrive home again. Fond memories beat bills any day.

If you plan to go fishing and are over the age of fifteen,

you'll need to buy a license (see chapter 7, Activities).There's a tax of 11.225 percent on show tickets. When you order those tickets from a show ticket agency, you'll most likely have to pay fees of at least $2 per ticket. Some agencies also have drop-off services and will leave the tickets at your hotel for an additional fee. Though this doesn't seem like a service that most of us (who are watching our money) would buy, there may be occasions when time is more important to you than money.

Then there are the taxes and surcharges. Branson hotel room taxes are 11.225 percent of the bill; taxes on meals served in restaurants are 7.725 percent. If you rent a car at Springfield/Branson Regional Airport, in addition to the rental price you'll pay a 10 to 11.1 percent tax for airport concession fee recovery, a per-day charge of $1.88 for vehicle license and property (other agencies may charge 1.35 percent in lieu of the per diem), and 6.47 percent sales tax, or a total of from 17.82 to 18.45 percent.

Pay Telephone Pointers

Once upon a time, you could be virtually positive that a long-distance phone call from a pay telephone would cost less than it would if placed from your hotel or motel room. Since deregulation, large telephone service providers make business arrangements with various vendors to service groups of machines. What the vendors charge, for use of the phones, can range from reasonable to astronomical. One employee of a large telephone service provider reported that she had seen charges of up to $30 for a three-minute long-distance call from a pay phone.

Budgets vary so greatly that we don't want to go into any specifics as to what you can expect to spend per day. We do, however, urge you to be realistic. It will cost much more if you neglect to bring along sufficient funds, ATM cards, or traveler's checks and have to rely on credit card advances. Rates listed on cash advance machines range from around $7 to $10 for amounts up to $200. We also recommend that you bring along more than one ATM card, since not all machines accept every kind. If you have a card issued by a banking chain with a branch in Branson, you won't have to pay charges when you use its ATMs. Branson chain branches include Bank of America, Commerce Bank, Firstar Bank, Great Southern Bank (two locations), Ozark Mountain Bank (five locations), and Union Planters Bank.

PRACTICAL PACKING

Needless to say, your mode of transportation will influence the amount of luggage you take on your Branson trip. The main thing to remember is to keep it simple. Although the performers in the shows wear fairly extravagant costumes, their audiences are dressed for comfort. Casual attire is the fashion—you may see a sport coat now and then, but not often. Slacks and knit tops, sundresses, and shorts will take you anywhere in summer. Since residents of the southern Missouri/ northern Arkansas area tend to be Bible Belt conservative, bikinis should be saved for poolside. Long pants, warm shirts, and a windbreaker will keep you comfortable during the cooler days of spring and fall. In the coldest days of winter, however, you'll be happier with long johns, a warm jacket, cap, and gloves.

Anytime you visit, bring along a sweater. Since the showrooms and most restaurants are air-conditioned, it can be cool inside even on the warmest of days. Bring sunscreen, too. And don't forget those comfortable shoes. Moleskin is important for people who tend to get blisters on their feet. Putting pieces of moleskin on the tender spots *before* they blister eliminates a lot of potential pain and suffering.

Speaking of health products, be sure to pack a few Band-Aids, safety pins, aspirins, and other small items that cost a lot more if you have to buy them from hotel dispensing machines or take the time to hunt for a drugstore. Tuck in an extra toothbrush or two if you'll be overnighting at more than one place— it's cheap insurance in case someone discovers she's forgotten hers at the last night's motel.

To minimize unpacking time, place such items as accessories, underwear, and socks in gallon-sized plastic bags with zip closings. If you don't have a separate container for toiletries, use plastic bags for them, too.

When you're taking a commercial tour, especially one with itineraries that depart from the hotel after breakfast and don't return until 10 or 11 P.M., savvy packing is crucial. Avoid garments with tight armholes. Pants with expandable waists are more comfortable if you have to wear them all day long. Garments in dark colors or patterns that don't show spills are far more practical than those that stain easily. You'll also want to be able to dress in layers, since it's usually a good deal cooler in early morning—and sometimes in the evening—than it is in the middle of the day. You might also consider those handy slacks with zip-off legs so they can be converted into shorts.

You'll also want to carry along an over-the-shoulder bag or small duffel for the day's purchases, your camera, and perhaps an extra pair of shoes—or even slippers if your feet swell during hot weather. Most motorcoach tours make provision for participants to leave items on the bus while they're visiting attractions, eating meals, and attending shows.

My favorite garments for nonstop days when I won't see my hotel room from dawn to midnight are wrinkle-free shirts, pants, and lightweight jackets with plenty of pockets—at least one of which has a zipper or Velcro closing. I also consider it a plus if there's a zipper pocket large enough to accommodate a point-and-shoot camera.

To save more money and time if you're traveling by car, bring along an ice chest. Having food in the car, ready to eat, means you don't have to take time off from sight-seeing to stop and buy snacks. Even if you don't use it for snacks or lunch or breakfast foods (see chapter 3), you'll want to keep bottled water and other beverages cold in the chest—a twelve-pack of soft drinks costs from two to five times less than the price of the same number of drinks bought individually.

Whereas car and RV travelers can always find a place to put their purchases, bus and airplane travelers should remember to bring an empty carry-on in order to have packing room for items they can't resist buying. Pack an extra pair of eyeglasses and prescriptions for any medications you might need.

Solo travelers may also want to bring a book along to discourage excessively chatty seatmates on planes and tour buses and for passing the time waiting in lines.

One of the best Branson Web sites is www.bestreadguides. com. In addition to information on accommodations, dining, shows, and attractions—as well as the current weather—there are discount coupons that can be printed and clipped. Among those offered in 2001 were a buy-one, get-one lunch buffet or lunch special at Whipper-Snappers Restaurant; $5 off on a $25 purchase at the two Kitchen Collection outlets; and discount coupons for various shows, including Jim Stafford Theatre and Bart Rockett, Magician.

When you're in Branson, you can dial the twenty-four-hour automated B-Line, which provides information on local weather and events taking place. It also has information about half a dozen restaurants, various shops, and attractions, and about thirty shows that subscribe to the service.

Radio station KRZK (106.3 FM) advertises itself as "Branson's Hometown Country Station," playing country music and four weather reports each hour. The TV Vacation Channel provides sneak previews of music shows and information on the most convenient travel routes in town. And if you tire of listening to country music, tune to KSMU, the public radio station at 91.1 FM on your dial.

2

Branson Bedtime

When you're going to stay in a hotel room for only one night, almost anything will do as long as it's clean, doesn't smell, and has a decent bed. When you're booked in for three or four or seven days, however, you want to get full value for your money. After all, accommodations take the biggest chunk out of most vacation budgets.

That's why I'm always amazed when people don't ask the questions they should before booking. Furthermore, they obligingly agree to the first price quoted, without inquiring whether there are any discounts or packages available.

Some of the questions that can help you get the room you'll be happiest in include:

- Are all rooms in the same price range identical in size and amenities?

- Do rooms with a view cost more than those that look out on the parking lot?

- Do quiet rooms cost more than those backed up to the elevator shaft or the highway?

- Are nonsmoking rooms occasionally rented out to smokers or are they always reserved for people who don't smoke? We recently stayed in a room that was supposedly nonsmoking.

There were, however, ashtrays on the nightstand and table. When we returned home, we noticed that the clean clothes we had not worn smelled of cigarette smoke.

- Is someone available to carry luggage? (This is extremely important to people who have bad backs.)
- Is there room service or a restaurant on the premises? If not, how far away are food service facilities?
- Are there sidewalks or maintained paths suitable for taking walks in the area?
- Is there a children's play area nearby? Can hotel personnel provide names of bonded child care professionals?
- How many shows and attractions are within a walking distance that's comfortable for most people?
- If the property is on more than one floor, is there an elevator?
- What percentage of the guests are members of tour groups? Business travelers?

The last question is an important one when you're looking for bargains, since hotels and motels that derive a significant portion of their revenue from tour groups and business travelers obviously can afford to discount and still make a profit.

Even if they cater primarily to individual leisure travelers, almost every lodging place has a fair amount of room between its rack (published) rate and the lowest amount of money the front desk people will accept to get their rooms rented. I didn't realize quite how much room some of them have, however, until I recently checked into a nationally franchised motor hotel. The rack rate was $149. I settled for a promotional rate of $79.99. While I was at the reception desk, the man to my right, who works for a state-affiliated utility, got *his* room for $43! Had I bargained a little more strenuously, I probably could have chopped another $20 off my bill, because it was late and the property wasn't close to full. You can easily do better than I did if you're willing to put in the effort.

When you have lots of lead time, phone toll-free numbers

for several Branson hotels, motels, or other lodging possibilities that sound good to you. Ask about discounts, packages, and promotions that will be in effect during your stay (ask them to send brochures, too). Several lodging chains, such as Holiday Inn, offer promotions on a more or less ongoing basis, such as Best Breaks. Not all of the hotels participate in a chain's promotions, but phoning their toll-free numbers can save you money if they do.

Most of the time, promotions and packages will lower the price you have to pay. When the rate isn't lowered, the packages will include extras. Reject those packages whose extras aren't of value to you and consider those that are—if the price is right. The typical Branson accommodations package includes show tickets and perhaps a meal or two.

By comparing the total package prices with the separate elements (request rate cards from the lodging places that interest you and a show guide from the chamber of commerce), you can easily see if packages are good, great, or excellent bargains. You may also find some nondeals. If you don't find any that fit your travel style or budget, you might also telephone or write hotels and motels directly. True, phone calls and stamps cost money. But by contacting properties directly, you'll find out about deals that the people manning toll-free switchboards often don't have in their computers.

Be persistent. Memberships in automobile clubs such as AAA, professional organizations, or the American Association of Retired Persons (AARP), along with corporate tie-ins, can mean additional savings. Don't make any decisions until you have checked deals in the newspaper (chains such as Hilton and Radisson often advertise worldwide promotions in newspaper travel sections) and on the Internet as well. Then go with what sounds like the very best deal to you. Guarantee the reservation with your credit card, being sure to inquire about the cancellation policy. Most hotels will allow you to cancel up to 6 P.M. on the date of your first night's stay, but that isn't always so. You may find an even better deal before the cancellation deadline.

The majority of Branson's twenty-three thousand hotel and motel rooms have been built within the last ten years; most of them within the past five. This makes a difference, especially in rooms that fall into the economy class, where wear and tear become most conspicuous.

You'll no doubt notice that we make no attempt to rank same-price hotels, motels, condos, or other lodging places. The reasons for this are simple. Management changes, employees come and go, so the conditions that prevail one week won't necessarily be the same the following. Also, decor is a subjective thing; our taste may not necessarily coincide with yours. As an alternative to the ranking system, we try to point you in the direction of properties that we think—at the time this book is written—offer good value for the money. In the process, we've undoubtedly omitted some great deals, and we hope you'll let us know about them so they can be included in the next edition.

LODGING CHAINS

Almost all of the major lodging chains in the economy and moderate categories now are represented in Branson. You can telephone them directly or call toll-free numbers to find out about their packages and promotions. Most of these chains have Internet sites as well. Among the chains with properties in Branson are:

Comfort Inn	800/228-5150 or 417/335-4727
Days Inn	800/324-4191 or 417/334-5544
Econo Lodge	800/553-2666 or 417/336-4849
Fairfield Inn	800/228-2800 or 417/336-5665
Hampton Inn	800/426-7866 or 417/334-6500
Hampton Inn West	
	800/426-7866 or 417/337-5762
Holiday Inn Express (Main)	
	800/465-4329 or 417/334-1985
Holiday Inn Express	
	800/465-4329 or 417/336-2100
Howard Johnson	888/336-3212 or 417/336-5151
Marriott (Residence Inn)	
	800/331-3131 or 417/336-4077

Quality Inn & Suites
              800/228-5151 or 417/334-1194
Quality Inn Branson
              800/228-5151 or 417/335-6776
Radisson Hotels   800/333-3333 or 417/335-5767
Ramada Inn
    800/641-4106, 800/856-0730, or 417/337-5207
Red Roof Inn   800/351-4644 or 417/335-4500
Rodeway Inn   800/228-2000 or 417/334-8694
Shoney's Inn & Suites
              800/633-6603 or 417/336-1100
Shoney's Southern Oaks Inn
              800/633-6603 or 417/335-8108
Sleep Inn   800/753-3746 or 417/336-3770
Super 8   800/343-2769 or 417/272-8195
Travelodge   800/578-7878 or 417/334-8300

Hampton Inn West (3695 West 76 Country Music Boulevard; 800/426-7866 or 417/337-5762) guarantees "If you're not
100% satisfied with your stay, we don't expect you to pay." The
Hampton room rate includes continental breakfast of muffins,
doughnuts, cereal, fruit, juices, coffee, and tea. There's an indoor pool and guest laundry in the facility, which is within
walking distance of eleven hotels and ten restaurants. The
hotel was built in 1984; its rack rate is $73 per night double.
Another property in the same chain, Hampton Inn Central, is
located at 2350 Green Mountain Drive (800/443-6504 or 417/
334-6500). Among Hampton Inn's promotions nationwide in
2001 was "Get a $10 e-coupon for your favorite retailers when
you make your registration online."
    Quality Inn's (800/245-3308) Exciting Escape is its least
expensive package. The two-night stay includes the choice of
one attraction, one show, and complimentary breakfast each
day for $79.50 per person. The three-night Ozark Fun package
includes lodging; choice of show; a ticket to either Silver Dollar City, the Dixie Stampede, or a *Branson Belle* cruise; complimentary breakfasts; and a $25 dinner certificate for $139.50
per person. Other two- to five-night packages consist of Quality Inn accommodations and two to six shows. These packages

range in price from about $199 to $522 per couple, excluding tax.

Howard Johnson (3027A West Highway 76; 800/I-GO-HOJO or 417/336-5151) is a 345-room motor hotel that won the Branson 2000 Hotel of the Year award. Among its amenities are an outdoor pool, playground, free deluxe continental breakfasts, data ports, cable TV, and free local calls. It's also within a mile of twenty theaters.

Days Inn (3524 Keeter Street; 888/334-7858 or 417/334-5544), which advertises fifteen shows at theaters within a mile of its location, provides a free continental breakfast and has a large pool complex as well as a kiddies' playground.

In 2001, **Howard Johnson** and **Days Inn** offered a variety of packages including Thrill Seeker Get Away Adventure at $290 per person double occupancy. The Thrill Seeker featured a half-day guided kayak tour on Table Rock Lake or Lake Taneycomo and a half-day guided mountain bike tour in Ozark Mountain country. Both tours included instruction, equipment, and transportation. The package also provided two nights' lodging at Days Inn or Howard Johnson plus a dinner show.

Among other packages with Days Inn or Howard Johnson accommodations, the two-night Family Fun in the Sun package featured tickets to the Dixie Stampede show and a visit to Silver Dollar City with a four-course meal ($373 per couple; $79 per child ages twelve through seventeen; and $49 per child ages three through eleven). Two-, three-, and four-night packages with three, four, and five shows, respectively, sold for $185, $255, and $299 per person. In August, a special offered on the Internet called Family Fun Getaway included two nights' lodging at Days Inn, an all-you-can-eat buffet dinner, tickets to the Magnificent 7 Show, and All Day Super Passes to Branson USA amusement park. The $242 price was based on a family of four consisting of two adults and two children.

Almost every hotel and motel in Branson offers specials. Whether they appeal to you depends on your interests and whether you're traveling alone, as a couple, with friends, or with a family, and the ages of those in your party. Several properties in Branson cater to seniors, others to the family trade. For example, kids eighteen years and under stay free in their parents' rooms at **Fairfield Inn** (220 Highway 165 South; 800/334-4386 or 417/336-5665). The $62 rate in 2001 included complimentary continental breakfast and free local phone calls.

The two **Holiday Inn Express** properties in Branson (1000 West Main, 800/465-4329 or 417/334-1985; and 2801 Green Mountain Drive, 417/336-2100) provide in-room coffeemakers, hair dryers, irons and ironing boards, an indoor pool, sauna, and fitness room. There's also a complimentary continental breakfast that includes four cereals, English muffins, toast, doughnuts, fruit, juice, and coffee. Both properties have a Best Breaks rate that you must ask for at the time of booking. The variable rate is based on availability and set by each of the properties in the chain.

Several motels are affiliated with Best Western, and while they generally aren't as predictable as the chain motels and hotels, quality is almost always above average. Three of Branson's **Best Western** motels—**Best Western Branson, Barrington Hotel,** and **Branson Towers**—offer their guests free shuttle service to and from the Red Roof Mall, Tanger Mall, Factory Stores of America, and downtown Branson. These three properties also provide free deluxe continental breakfasts and local phone calls.

In the higher-end price range of chains is **Marriott Residence Inn** (280 Wildwood Drive; 800/331-3131 or 417/336-4077), which offers a total of eighty-five one-bedroom, two-bedroom, and studio suites, some of which have fireplaces. They come with fully equipped kitchens, and the price includes such amenities as complimentary breakfasts, an indoor pool and spa, complimentary newspaper, exercise room, guest laundry, and complimentary grocery shopping. There's also an outdoor basketball court on the premises and an eighteen-hole golf course across the street.

The ten-story **Radisson Hotel** (120 South Wildwood Drive; 800/333-3333 or 417/335-5767), with more than five hundred rooms, has an indoor/outdoor pool, a fitness center with sauna, and a beauty salon. Guest rooms have iron and ironing board and hair dryers as well as the usual amenities such as coffeemakers. Twenty-seven suites occupy the concierge level on the ninth floor, where complimentary continental breakfast, cocktails, and hors d'oeuvres are served. Among the Radisson's packages are Escape, which includes one night's deluxe accommodations and full breakfast for two as well as two tickets to the show or attraction of the guests' choice for $159. The three-night Escape package, which includes two shows or attractions, sells for $407. The one-night Escape package with a Jacuzzi suite on the concierge level costs $214.

ONE-OF-A-KIND PROPERTIES

Frankly speaking, the majority of Branson's motels are of the cookie-cutter variety (photos in two properties' brochures even show the same bedspreads in their guest rooms). When you book into one of these look-alikes, it's a good idea to have the name of the place where you're staying in your pocket. But if you want to stay in places set apart by their individuality, you will be able to find these, too.

Take the **Branson Lodge**, for example, where all the guest rooms are furnished with antiques. You can buy any of the furnishings you take a fancy to. And talk about lowering the rates: If you mention their Web site, www.bransonlodge.com, you can get 40 percent off between January 1 and March 31, 30 percent off from April 1 through June 30, and 20 percent off the rest of the year.

The southern-style **Plantation Inn** (3460 West Highway 76; 800/417-5253 or 417/334-3600) in 2001 offered four set price packages in addition to those that were custom-tailored. Of the four, the least expensive—at $279 plus taxes per couple—included two nights' lodging at the hotel, four breakfasts, and two dinners, plus two tickets each to the Jim Stafford and Mickey Gilley shows. The most expensive, with six nights' lodging, included twelve breakfasts, four dinners, and two tickets to the Mel Tillis, Shoji Tabuchi, Barbara Fairchild, Baldknobbers, Mickey Gilley, Jim Stafford, and Country Tonite shows as well as two tickets to the *Showboat Branson Belle* Dinner Cruise ($959 plus tax per couple).

THEATER HOTELS

There's a good deal to be said for staying at one of Branson's theater hotels, which have been built in conjunction with theaters or are in close proximity of the theaters in which shows play. Not only do you save money in transportation costs, you save both time and frustration when your destination is just a short walk away.

In a quiet setting three miles south of Highway 76, the **Welk Resort Center and Champagne Theatre** (1984 Highway 165; 800/935-5431 or 417/337-7469) includes a four-story hotel with cable TV, pool, spa, guest laundry, and pet rooms. Complimentary continental breakfast is served daily, and there is free minigolf as well as a children's playground. The resort offers such specials as the Branson VIP Package—four nights' lodging plus the choice of four attractions, which include top shows, Silver Dollar City, and a cruise on the *Showboat Branson Belle*. Package prices vary with the season.

A vacation special advertised in the 2001 AAA tour book at $219 per person double occupancy included three nights at the Welk Resort Hotel, tickets to the Lawrence Welk Show, an all-you-can-eat buffet dinner or lunch, tickets to the Lennon Brothers Swing Music Show (with full breakfast), free continental breakfasts daily, tickets to two other shows (the choices included Mel Tillis, the Osmonds, Jim Stafford, Shoji Tabuchi, Yakov Smirnoff, and Bobby Vinton), plus discount coupons to Branson's outlet malls, and souvenir postcards.

The regular double room rate listed in the tour book was $94 to $99 for two people in a double room, which would translate to $47 to $49.50 per person per night. Tickets to the Lawrence Welk Show cost $29.98; to the Lennon Brothers Swing Music Show, $25.53. Prices for the shows on the list of choices range from $27.50 to $31. Buying the package, savings per person for room and shows alone would be from $32.50 to $45, depending on which optional shows were chosen.

Grand Country Inn (1945 West 76 Country Boulevard; 800/828-9068 or 417/335-3535), formerly called the 76 Mall Inn, is part of the Grand Country Mall complex, which includes the Music Hall Theater. Hotel guests have access to miniature golf, a video game room with Ping-Pong and pool tables, outlet shopping, and free entry to Splash Country Water Park.

Palace Inn (2820 West Highway 76; 800/725-2236 or 417/ 334-7666), adjacent to the Grand Village and Grand Palace Theatre, has a restaurant, a gift shop, and beauty salon on site. The 166-room hotel is among the newer properties, and its central location close to a dozen or more theaters is a plus for people who want to do minimum driving. Golf packages are available, as are accommodations/show combination deals.

The **Baldknobbers Complex** consists of the **Baldknobbers Motor Inn,** the **Baldknobbers Theatre,** and the **Baldknobbers Restaurant** (2843 West Highway 76; 417/334-7948). Included in the motor inn rates are complimentary breakfasts and free local calls. Children stay free in parents' rooms; there's a gift shop on the premises. Among the 2001 Baldknobbers specials was one that featured two tickets to the Baldknobbers Jamboree show, two dinners at the Baldknobbers Restaurant, and one night's lodging for two at the Baldknobbers Motor Inn for $99.

CONDOMINIUMS

Many people have chosen condominium ownership so as to have a second home in the Branson area and earn some income off their investments as well. They use their vacation homes for varying amounts of time, and arrange for rental agencies rent them out the rest of the year. When time-share operations have vacant condos, they also rent them out to tourists. Many condominiums require minimum seven-day rentals during summer, fall foliage season, and other busy times of the year. However, it is possible to rent condos on a two-night minimum basis or even for a single night.

Some of the condominium units have great views and smart furnishings. But that's not always the case. Views may be of carport roofs; decor can be tasteless. Before you rent a condo for any significant period of time, request photos of both the exterior and interior of the unit you'll be renting.

Holiday Hills Resort & Golf Club (620 East Rockford

Drive; 800/225-2422 or 417/239-2700) rents one- to three-bed-room condominiums on a nightly basis. The condos surround an eighteen-hole championship golf course. There are also tennis, basketball, and shuffleboard courts on the grounds as well as a swimming pool. Holiday Hills 2001 Unlimited Golf Package ($396 for two people in a one-bedroom luxury condo for two nights and three days) included unlimited golf at Holi-day Hills, a $25 certificate to Grille on the Green restaurant, and a special gift box. Rack rate for the accommodations is $109 per night; the green fee for eighteen holes is $51 before 11 A.M. and $41 after.

Views from the one-, two-, and three-bedroom condomini-ums at **Pointe Royale** (158-A Pointe Royale Drive; 800/962-4710 or 417/334-5614) are of the Ozark Mountain bluffs, Lake Taneycomo, or the development's eighteen-hole golf course. Each of the units has a private patio or deck as well as a full kitchen.

Still Waters Condominium Resort (21 Stillwater Trail; 800/777-2320) on Table Rock Lake features three swimming pools plus a water flume slide, a game room, playground, and free use of paddleboats and bikes. Docks and a boat launch, along with pontoon, boat, and Jet Ski rentals, provide addi-tional recreational opportunities. There's even a ticket outlet on the premises. Regular rates run from $69 for a poolside studio with kitchenette during spring, fall, and winter to three-bedroom/two-bath lakefront cottages for $209 in summer. Specials, however, can bring those rates down to $59 and $109 (some of the units are much nicer than others).

The handsomely appointed condos at the **Village at Indian Point** (24 Village Trail; 800/984-7847 or 417/338-8801; www.branson.net/thevillage), with two bedrooms and two baths, sleep up to six people. Floor plans include living areas with stone fireplaces, dining areas, and large private covered decks. Some units have Jacuzzi tubs, washer/dryers, and VCRs as well as lake views. A horseshoe pit, barbecue area, dock, and fishing deck provide on-site recreational opportunities.

Indian Point Resorts entertainment packages for two peo-ple offer lakefront lodge units with kitchen, show tickets, and a Branson discount coupon book (an extra bedroom is included in the packages for four). Packages are for two, three, or five nights' accommodations, and tickets for any of forty different shows can be included. If additional room nights and/or shows are desired, they, too, are discounted. Prices vary with dates, room types, and shows selected. Indian Point also sells Crafts Festival, Children's Festival, and Holiday packages that tie in with the dates of these special events. Rates for accommodations at the Indian Point Resorts range from $69 to $89 for the least expensive lakefront lodge units to $220 to $290 for deluxe four-bedroom units at their most expensive property. Rates at the two other properties are slightly less.

Ozark Mountain Resort Swim and Tennis Club on the shores of Table Rock Lake (eighteen miles from Branson on Highway 13; 800/225-2422) is among the other popular condominium rental complexes.

BED-AND-BREAKFASTS

Although bed-and-breakfast establishments don't always offer the standard discounts such as AAA, available at most accommodations, most of them offer packages or discounted rates at some time during the year. Even without discounts, bed-and-breakfasts can provide good return for visitors who value personal attention.

Branson Hotel Bed and Breakfast (214 West Main; 800/933-0651 or 417/335-6104) was built in 1903 and completely restored in 1992 as an inn. Located in downtown Branson, it has seven rooms, so it's usually necessary to reserve well in advance. AAA and AARP discounts are available, and no minimum stay is required.

The sixteen-room **Bradford House Bed & Breakfast Inn** (296 Blue Meadows Road; 888/488-4445 or 417/334-4444) is located about ten minutes away from Missouri Highway 76 (Country Music Boulevard) with views of the Ozarks (some rooms have private access to the veranda). Double sinks and a video library are among the inn's amenities. Some suites are furnished with Jacuzzi whirlpool tubs, separate showers, and refrigerators.

The Victorian-style **Emory Creek Bed & Breakfast** (143 Arizona; 800/362-7404 or 417/337-7045) advertises gourmet breakfasts, live piano music, a garden with gazebo, and a nature trail on seven and a half acres.

Ozark Mountain Bed & Breakfast Service (P.O. Box 295, Branson; 800/695-1546; www.ozarkbedandbreakfast.com) handles reservations for a number of area bed-and-breakfast establishments ranging from turn-of-the-century Victorians to contemporary log lodges.

LAKESIDE LODGINGS

If you like views of the water, you'll want to investigate the accommodations overlooking Table Rock Lake. It does take a while to get to Branson when you want to shop or go to shows, but natural beauty and the smell of pine more than make up for your travel time.

The majority of Table Rock accommodations in the Branson orbit are concentrated on Indian Point, the most extensively developed resort area on the lake. The choice of lodgings ranges from condominium complexes with golf courses and marinas to rustic cabins and several motor hotels that overlook the water.

One of the nicest motor hotels on Indian Point is **Bradford Inn on the Lake** (800/864-6811). The rooms are fresh, cheerful, and more attractively decorated than most area properties. The balconies, looking out on the water, are large enough for two people to sit comfortably. The inn's sister properties, Bradford Inn and Bradford Inn Bed & Breakfast, are also described in this chapter.

While you're researching accommodations, be aware that lots of places that call themselves resorts aren't. There are a few resorts in the full-service sense of the word, of course. They have golf courses, tennis courts, marinas, and other amenities, but for the most part, resorts in the Branson area—as throughout Middle America—consist of clutches of rustic river- or lakeside cabins or cottages with a boat deck, a live-bait tank, and a couple of shelves next to the registration counter where fishing tackle, snacks, and sunscreen are for sale. They may well be delightful places to stay—just don't expect a concierge and spa.

Whether full-service resorts, cabins, cottages, condominiums, or campsites, you'll be able to find dozens of them on the shores of Table Rock Lake. You can find accommodations not listed in this book by inquiring at the Branson Chamber of Commerce or searching the Internet for Branson lake accommodations (search engine Google lists more than a hundred entries).

Luxury Lodgings

Although there are thousands of rooms in the midquality range, people looking for luxury may be disappointed, because deluxe digs are in short supply. But the most expensive hotels are often the ones that can afford to give the deepest discounts on their room prices.

Probably the fanciest accommodations in town are those at the AAA four-diamond **Chateau on the Lake** (415 North Highway 265; 888/333-5253 or 417/334-1161). The hotel, with more than three hundred rooms, features a ten-story atrium with an indoor waterfall, and overlooks Table Rock Lake. Four restaurants, indoor and outdoor pools, a day spa and salon, fitness center, and game room are among its attractions. Lakeshore facilities include a full-service marina with equipment for scuba diving, waterskiing, fishing, and other water sports available.

Big Cedar Lodge (612 Devil's Pool Road, Ridgedale; 417/335-2777) is another upscale charmer, with its spectacular views and first-class amenities. Set in a wooded area on the shores of Table Rock Lake, the complex includes a trio of separate lodge buildings: Adirondack-style Spring View Lodge, the cedar-and-limestone Valley View Lodge, and sixty-five-unit Falls Lodge, newest of the three. In addition, nine moss-green cottages and an assortment of private log cabins are nestled in the trees or along the lakeshore. There are five restaurants on the premises.

Lodge rooms for two range in price from $69 to $189 in low season to $125 to $289 in high season. There's also a daily

$10-per-person incidental services fee in spring, summer, and fall (it's $5 in winter), which includes unlimited access to the fitness center, unlimited local and long-distance telephone access, all incoming faxes, courtesy shuttle, unlimited use of canoes, paddleboats, and golf practice facilities, daily newspaper, miniature golf, concierge services, and a number of additional amenities.

That doesn't mean that everyone always pays full price. In addition to packages, on selected dates throughout the year, lodging units are discounted from 10 to 25 percent on a space-available basis.

Bradford Inn (on Highway 265, two miles south of Highway 76; 800/357-1466) is considered one of the best values for money spent as far as Branson lodging is concerned. The immaculate green-shuttered inn offers individually decorated guest rooms, a delightful setting, spectacular views (it's said that on a clear day they reach to fifty miles away), and sumptuous breakfasts. Some of the rooms have fireplaces; most of them have Jacuzzis and refrigerators. Private decks and patios, flower-filled window boxes, and a wooded setting add to the ambience.

WITHOUT RESERVATIONS

Although most Branson visitors make reservations in advance, there are times when that just isn't possible, or may not be practical. Say you get some unexpected time off and find a great deal on airfare. Perhaps you suddenly realize that you need a vacation and arrive in Branson without reservations. With a little bit of luck and effort, you can find deals. In fact, you can sometimes find the very best bargains available when you're on the spot.

For example, you might drop by the Welcome Center (269 Highway 248) to use the services of the Lodging Locator, a customized computer system that lists a selection of accommodations that have same-day vacancies. The computer matches preferred location, type of lodging, and desired price range to properties with vacancies. It also makes reservations and prints out driving directions. However, you can use it without making the reservations and use your bargaining skills to save money.

Take advantage of the Lodging Locator's information (it can be accessed after business hours by phoning 417/336-4466). Make a list of the places with vacancies that sound best to you. Then go personally to the hotel or motel at the top of your list and see if you can get a better rate than the one indicated on the Locator.

When you can't get a discount at the first hotel or motel on your list, go on to the next one. Chances are good—particularly in late afternoon, when there are a lot of unsold rooms in town—that lodging places will be eager to lower their rates when given a halfway legitimate reason to do so. Since room rates fluctuate with demand, they can move down as surely as they move up.

RECREATIONAL VEHICLE CAMPGROUNDS

The more than twelve hundred campsites in the Branson area are of two types—privately owned facilities and those operated by the U.S. Army Corps of Engineers. The fifteen Corps of Engineers recreation areas provide electricity, rest rooms, showers, dump stations, boat launches, and swimming areas. They are located in naturlaly pleasant places, with lots of trees—and sometimes a creek, river, or lake nearby.

Private facilities include **Branson City Campground** (300 South BoxCar Willie Drive; 417/334-2915) with 350 spaces on the river in a rather dismal setting not far from downtown. Most of the sites are full service, with handicapped access, cable TV, and picnic tables. **Branson KOA** (1025 Headwaters Road; 800/562-4177 or 417/334-7457), with 170 sites, an outdoor pool, and shuttle service among its amenities, has a more pleasant location away from congestion.

The privately owned campgrounds that follow either have convenient locations for people who like to be in the center of the action, have larger-than-average recreational vehicle parking spaces, and/or afford good views and shade trees. Unfortunately, most campgrounds don't have all these features.

Compton Ridge Campground (5040 Highway 265; 800/

233-8648), with 227 sites, is among the campgrounds with the most amenities and offers lovely surroundings. **Silver Dollar City Campground** (5125 Highway 265; 417/338-8189) is another pretty campground. It has 185 spaces, 110 of which provide full hook-ups. The campground's location at Silver Dollar City is handy for RVers whose main reason for a Branson trip is visiting the theme park.

Several smaller campgrounds are also located in the immediate Branson area. They include **Branson Shenanigans RV Park** (3675 Keeter Street; 800/338-7275 or 417/334-4785), with thirty sites; **Branson Stagecoach RV Park** (5751 Highway 165; 800/446-7110 or 417/335-8190), with fifty-two spaces; and **Deer Run Campgrounds** (1056 Indian Point Road; 800/908-3337 or 417/338-1020).

HOUSEBOAT HAVENS

During fine weather, you may find that renting a houseboat for your Branson stay provides not only delightful accommodations, but also a change-of-pace way of life. Table Rock Lake is warm enough that you can go swimming whenever you decide to. Fishing's an option, too. Barbecues on the deck. Sleeping under the stars rather than in the glow of the neon lights along Missouri Highway 76. And when you want to see the shows, they're just a short drive away.

There are two major houseboat rental companies. **Branson Houseboat Rentals/Forever Resorts** (Gage's Marina, 915 Long Creek, Ridgedale on Table Rock Lake; 800/255-5561 or 417/335-3042; www.foreverresorts.com) rents houseboats with four queen beds, a queen sofa sleeper, central heat and air-conditioning, TV/VCR, cassette stereo, full-sized range and oven, microwave, two refrigerators, gas grill, one and a half baths, and a five-hundred-square-foot sundeck with water slide.

Rates for houseboats that sleep ten people—the fifty-six-foot standard and sixty-five-foot VIP models—vary a good deal depending on the season. In 2001, the lowest rate for a standard houseboat was $995 for a three-day weekend or four days midweek during value season (January 1 through April 31; October 14 through December 31). It cost $1,695 weekly. The same houseboat rented for $1,395 ($1,995 weekly) during spring (May 1 through June 4) and fall seasons (September 2 through October 13), and $1,995 ($2,995 weekly) during the June 5 through September 1 regular season. VIP houseboats were $2,195 and $3,295 for value, spring, and fall seasons; $2,895 and $4,595 during regular season.

Tri Lakes Houseboat Rentals (49 Lake Road; 800/982-2628 or 441/739-2370; www.tri-lakeshouseboat.com) rents units that sleep four, six, ten, and twelve people. For food preparation, each houseboat is equipped with a propane barbecue grill, stove with oven and microwave, refrigerator, ice chest, coffeemaker, and toaster. Bedding, cookware, and other kitchen essentials are also included.

The ten-sleeper rented in 2001 for three nights at $971 ($1,733 weekly) in March or April; $1,121 ($2,000) in May or October; $1,270 ($2,266) June 1 through June 10 and during September; and $1,494 ($2,666) from June 11 through August. Houseboats that sleep four started at $437 ($781) during low season and rented for $673 ($1,201) during peak season.

But What About Fido?

One feature animal lovers will appreciate about **Ramada Ltd.** (2316 Shepherd of the Hills Expressway; 800/856-0730 or 417/337-5207) is that their pets can stay with them for an extra $5 a night. Several other Branson motels also allow animals, most of them requiring a damage deposit.

If you can't bear to leave your dog, cat, or parakeet at home and aren't able to find accommodations you like that allow your nonhuman friends to stay with you, make reservations for them at the **Branson Pet Resort** (417/335-6045; www.abka.com/branson). The facility caters to visiting canines by providing spacious quarters lined with lambskin. Cats enjoy lambskin-lined kitty condos. Birds are put up in luxury digs, too.

3

Maximizing Mealtime

Though the restaurant count in Branson stands at more than 350, there's a numbing sameness about most of their buffet and menu choices. "Set salads" (Jell-O with everything in it from pineapples, cottage cheese, and marshmallows to cashews, cherries, and cabbage); beef tips, pork ribs, and hickory-smoked ham; canned or frozen vegetables; and mashed potatoes with gravy are main meal staples (whether that's for dinner served at midday or at 6 P.M.).

Add the dozens of chain-linked Applebee's, McDonald's, Red Lobsters, Taco Bells, and their look-alikes and you'll probably come to the conclusion that though meals during a Branson vacation won't be expensive, they won't be memorable either.

Happily, that doesn't have to be the case—especially for visitors who use a bit of local lore, logic, and ingenuity. First of all, midwesterners know that you can't judge a restaurant by the way it looks on the outside. Some of the best-tasting food is produced in kitchens of eateries that have shabby exteriors. The interiors might not look so great, either, with maroon booths and orange Formica tables. So, when a restaurant has been recommended to you, don't cross it off your list just because it looks tired or tacky.

Instead, check out the parking lot for Missouri licenses in Branson license plate holders. Step inside and eyeball the clientele. It's fairly easy to tell the locals from tourists—especially when tour buses are parked cheek to jowl outside. A customer base made up of residents usually means that the food is good enough to make them come back for more.

Once you're inside and looking over the menu, take advantage of regional dishes, such as black-eyed peas, walleye pike with homemade tartar sauce, or stuffed pan-fried catfish. Foods that are indigenous to the area generally are good choices, too, so try the Missouri honey on fluffy buttermilk biscuits, the wild plum cobbler, and fresh blackberry pie. Remember, too, that you're in a state where cooking has been influenced by the South, even though it's not technically a southern state. So expect to find lots of okra in the vegetable soup, corn bread muffins, and southern fried chicken.

By the way, when seeking recommendations, forget about asking opinions of people at hotel front desks and others in the hospitality industry. Instead, ask salespeople at bookstores, small-business managers, and other locals where they go for a good meal. If you do ask hospitality industry employees' opinions, personalize your questions. Ask them where *they* like to go on special occasions.

SCOUTING THE BUFFETS

Buffets are the mainstay of the Branson dining scene. Macaroni salad. Three-bean salad. Beet pickles. Chicken à la king. Tuna hot-dish. Beef stew. Beef ribs. Creamed peas. Lima beans and ham—the litany of buffet items is fairly standard. But for people who love food in abundance, Branson buffets are magic carpets (or more accurately, tablecloths) laden with everything from comfort foods to an occasional ethnic dish. The philosophy of the buffet is to offer a variety of food, properly prepared and attractively presented. At a buffet, more than in any other dining environment, people eat with their eyes as well as their stomachs.

Wherever a buffet is, whatever the items on the table, buffet mavens agree that to maximize your dining experience, it's important to have a strategy. One plan of attack is to take a portion of each dish, trying to fit them all onto one plate. But unless you like the cherry Jell-O oozing into the pickled cucumbers and coleslaw mixing with the fruit salad, this method is not recommended. A better idea is to walk around the buffet table, making mental note of what you would really like to eat. Then pick up your plate and stick to your choices.

Another buffet technique is to select a tiny portion of each of five salads, keeping them isolated from each other on the plate. Then decide which one you like best and go back for a larger portion. Proceed through the entrées in the same fashion. Then take one or two desserts that look most tempting.

While some buffets urge patrons to eat all they want, it isn't cricket to take food with you when you leave. Some of the establishments have signs reminding patrons that they should take only what they can eat. At others, waitresses quietly speak to people who are seen slipping food into pockets and purses.

Perhaps the most compelling attraction of a buffet is that there no rules as to what you must eat. If you adore Spanish rice or danish pastries, you don't have to eat anything but. No veggies. No fruit. And as to sequence, forget the "finish your meat and potatoes." If you feel that life is uncertain, eat dessert first.

The following is only a partial list of the buffets offered in Branson, based on surroundings and serving tables that looked good or were recommended to us:

Stage Door Canteen (Lawrence Welk Champagne Theatre; 417/337-7469) is decorated like someone's vision of an army canteen during World War II and the Korean conflict (it has pink walls). The breakfast buffets are the best of the three meals offered here, according to people who bought a Welk resort package and ate there three days in a row.

Penelope's Family Restaurant (3015 Highway 76; 417/334-335) claims to make just about everything from scratch—take helpings of the meat loaf and mashed potatoes for proof. The buffet tables are heavily weighted toward desserts such as berry cobblers and carrot cake.

The Golden Corral (3551 Shepherd of the Hills Expressway; 417/336-6297) gets high marks for its buffets from people who have lived in Branson for years (the $1 discount tickets in entertainment publications are widely distributed).

At **The Rails** (433 Animal Safari Road; 417-336/3401), you can eat your fill of fish and seafood for less than $10. There are chicken and ribs in addition to the clam chowder, seafood gumbo, stuffed crab, and other crustacean creations at this buffet. Good desserts, too.

Peppercorn's Restaurant and Bakery (2421 Highway 76; 417/335-6699) has an especially popular breakfast buffet, which includes a fresh fruit bar as well as homemade cinnamon rolls and hot muffins in addition to the usual buffet fare. The variety of salad bar ingredients at the lunch and dinner buffets is a big draw, too.

At **Hong Kong Buffet** (1206 Highway 76; 417/334-2727) you'll be able to choose from chow mein, broccoli beef, egg rolls, and a hundred other Chinese dishes for a modest price. There are other Oriental buffets in town, too. **Tran's Chinese Buffet** (1305 Highway 76; 417/334-4652) offers Chinese dishes with a definite Vietnamese flavor; **Lotus Valley** (3129 Highway 76; 417/334-3427; a 10 percent off coupon is available) features low-fat dishes as well as the regular Chinese buffet fare.

The Hard Work U buffet, served only on Sunday at the College of the Ozarks' **Friendship House** (at the entrance gates; 417/334-6411), includes roast beef, ham, fried chicken, a meat entrée, a casserole, potatoes, candied yams, green beans, corn, a full salad bar, home-baked desserts, and homemade bread. Though this buffet doesn't include as many dishes as most others, the food is very well prepared.

The setting for the Sunday champagne brunch at Big Cedar Lodge (612 Devil's Pool Road, Ridgedale; 417/335-5141) is the **Worman House Restaurant,** formerly the elegant country retreat of a Frisco Railroad executive named Harry Worman and his wife. Granted, the $24.95 price puts this buffet in the splurge category, and the resort involves a bit of a drive. However, the food (tomatoes stuffed with pine nuts and other unusual ingredients; osso buco and broccoli rissoto), the ambience, and the surroundings as you take a postbuffet stroll around the grounds will make you feel like royalty.

SIT-DOWN DINING

The restaurants that follow were chosen because they offer something   out-of-the-Branson-ordinary—better-than-usual food, especially attractive or clever decor, or an ambience that sets them apart from the rest. We have included restaurants that offer bargains in the form of specials, promotions, and discount coupons as well as some high-end restaurants that are bargains simply because you would pay much more for what you get in any other popular vacation area.

Donovan's Hillbilly Inn (1176 West Highway 76; 417/334-6644) advertises "Branson's Best Meat and Eggs Breakfast." Although it definitely isn't for folks watching their calories or cholesterol, the meal is indeed hearty enough to keep most people going until dinnertime. The basics consist of two eggs, any style, and either whole-hog sausage patties, hickory- and sassafras-smoked ham and redeye gravy, or bacon. They're served with country-fried potatoes, hash browns, or grits, plus biscuits and gravy or toast with apple butter, grape jelly, Missouri bee honey, and sorghum. There's an even bigger breakfast that adds fruit juice, sugar-and-cinnamon-spiced apples, and coffee served with half-and-half.

At **Hard Luck Diner** (Grand Village Shops, 2800 West Highway 76; 417/336-7217) the hosts, servers, cooks, and cashiers burst into song whenever the microphone isn't being used by anyone else. Many of the performers have made tapes and CDs, which are for sale at the restaurant. Others are young adults hoping to break into show business. And they're surprisingly good. The food is good, too. Malts are made in the old-fashioned mixers and served in their metal containers. The french fries are the best I have ever tasted. The decor is pleasing, too. Hard Luck Diner coupons include a "kids eat free"—one child's meal with each adult meal purchased.

McFarlain's (inside the IMAX Entertainment Complex at 3562 Shepherd of the Hills Expressway; 417/336-4680) is another good place for lunch. The ambience is attractive with high-beamed ceilings and knotty-pine walls as well as pine tables, chairs, and booths. If you've never eaten fried sweet potatoes and fried green tomatoes, this is the place to try them. You'll probably need a friend to help you finish them, however, as the basket containing a combination of the two ($4.99) is huge. The green tomatoes are served with McFarlain's own ranch dressing; the sweet potatoes are accompanied by "calypso" sauce, made with coconut, brown sugar, pineapple, corn syrup, gingerroot, and cayenne. Other menu items include chicken potpie, Ozark noodle bake (lasagna), and pioneer pot roast. McFarlain's coupons include a "buy one breakfast, get second for half price" offer, as well as "pioneer pot roast dinner for two" at $15.99.

Another alternative to same-o, same-o dining is the **Friendship House** (entrance of the College of the Ozarks campus, two miles south of Branson off Highway 65; 417/334-6411). The food is prepared and served by students in white shirts, black pants or skirts, and wine-colored aprons, matching exactly the wine, black, and white booths and tables with their white linen cloths. Menu choices include such "Major Courses" as catfish fillets ($8.35) and rib eye steak ($10.35). "Campus Classics" like the ham and Swiss cheese deli sandwich, served with dinner salad or a cup of soup ($4.65), and "Sweet Finals," such as cheesecake ($2.35) and pecan pie ($1.99), aren't fancy, but are very well prepared and served.

Mary Jane's (one mile south of the West Highway 76 and Highway 13 junction; 417/272-8908) is an unexpected delight in West Branson. Reminiscent of a cottage in the English countryside, this is a place doting aunts take their nieces for special occasions. Open for lunch only, the restaurant's bill of fare includes quiche and crab salad sandwiches. Reservations are accepted.

Casa Fuentes (1107 West Highway 76; 417/339-3888) is located in a plain white house with a big red, white, and green sign that's hard to miss. Which is a good thing, because the restaurant is one of only a few genuine ethnic eateries in Branson. The menu lists just about every Mexican dish that most of us have ever tasted—plus several others. In addition to the usual tacos, tamales, enchiladas, and fajitas, you'll be able to order Bisteck à la Mexicana (beef tips stir-fried with tomatoes, onions, and jalapeño peppers, served with guacamole and sour cream), Pollo Poblano (chicken tenders covered with mole sauce), Senora Tinga (shredded beef brisket with tomatoes, onions, and chipotle peppers), and Pastel Indio (three layers of tortillas filled with chicken and cheese, covered with enchilada sauce). If you have room, try the flan for dessert.

The most expensive entrée on the dinner menu is the fajitas at $9.95. The least expensive entrées at dinner cost $4.95, which is also the price of the most expensive luncheon specials. Combination plates start at $5.95.

BT Bones (Shepherd of the Hills Expressway at Gretna Road; 417/335-2002) has a reputation for some of the best ribs around. Other menu items include prime rib, fajitas, grilled catfish, and trout. The big pluses, however, are that it's one of the only eating places where there's dancing in the evening as well as live country and western music performed by local musicians.

Lone Star Steakhouse (201 Wildwood Drive at Green Mountain Drive; 417/336-5038) is another western-themed restaurant, where every so often the waiters and waitresses line dance in the aisles. It's definitely a restaurant that appeals to a younger crowd during the afternoons and late evenings, but you'll see lots of seniors queueing up at dinnertime. Mesquite-grilled steaks are a specialty, as is smoked prime rib. You can also order from a selection of several combos, including a beef and a salmon fillet.

Blue-roofed **Shogun** (1962 Highway 165; 417/336-2244) is a Japanese steakhouse with U-shaped hibachi tables seating up to sixteen people. Chefs prepare each table's sukiyaki, teriyaki, tepanyaki, and other traditional dishes on plate steel grills set in the tables that can be heated to 425 degrees. Diners can also sit at conventional tables and order from the menu. Since Shogun's sushi is spectacular, you might select a third option—sitting at its sushi bar. More than a hundred varieties of the delectable fish and rice rolls are in the chefs' repertoires, according to a restaurant spokesman. Reservations are recommended; coupons for $1 off lunch and $1.50 off dinner are easy to find.

Sadie's Sideboard (2830 West Highway 76; 417/334-3619) is located in a perky yellow house set back from the busy highway. Although the restaurant serves buffet-style meals, you can also order such entrées as brisket, rib platter, and hickory-smoked ham from the menu. The atmosphere is cheerful, and the food gets good marks from the locals. Coupons we found offered "buy one adult buffet and get $2 off the second."

Branson Café (120 West Main Street; 417/334-3021) is a typical downtown Middle American restaurant with a twist. So many tourists have found out about it that the locals don't turn their heads to look at the strangers anymore. Most of the waitresses have been around for ages; the pies are made by the boss, who has been making them there for fourteen years. Not only does he make cherry, apple, raisin, fresh strawberry, pecan, pineapple, and custard pies, but he makes five kinds of cream pies and cobblers with five different fillings, too.

If you're at the Branson Café for breakfast, you won't go wrong with the one egg, any style, that comes with light-as-air biscuits and a huge helping of very good fried potatoes—all for $2.85. Coffee drinkers will want to add a "bottomless" cup of fresh-ground coffee ($.90).

The Shack Café (108 South Commercial Street; 417/334-3490) is another Branson old-timer—in fact, it's the oldest restaurant in town. Waitresses still put your order on the cook's spin wheel and carry a running conversation with the regular customers. If you grew up in a small town in the heart of America, I guarantee you'll get a dollop of nostalgia along with the pot roast and raisin cream pie.

Farmhouse Restaurant (119 West Main Street; 417/334-9701) is open longer hours—7 A.M. until midnight, than most Branson eateries. House specialties are chicken-fried steak and blackberry cobbler, but there are daily specials as well. *Tip:* If you've had your fill of blackberry cobblers during your Branson stay and still aren't counting calories, try an apple dumpling with cinnamon ice cream for dessert.

The dishes at Pzazz (158 Pointe Royale Drive; 417/335-2798) have sports-inspired names. And no wonder: The owner-operator of the eatery is Jack Hamilton, who pitched in the majors for twenty years. Even the restaurant's location is sports-related—it overlooks the golf course at the Pointe Royale development. Menu choices range from prime rib pizza to fajitas, and you can eat while watching ESPN on big-screen TV.

Dockers Restaurant & Sports Bar (3100 Green Mountain Drive; 417/332-0044) appeals primarily to a younger crowd. The boat-shaped restaurant, in addition to a huge breakfast buffet, a lunch soup and salad bar, and dinnertime seafood and country buffets, offers menu dining with entrées such as BBQ ribs and catfish. When the restaurant is closed during midafternoon, head for the Sports Bar where sandwiches, pizza, and other snacks are always available. Several Dockers coupons are available (we found four different offers).

Landry's Seafood House (2900 West Highway 76; 417/339-1010), with its weathered-looking exterior, seems more like an East Coast restaurant than part of a Texas chain. The most expensive entrée on the menu is the seafood platter, at $17.99. Other offerings that get raves are the gumbo (it's spicy), stuffed flounder, lemon pepper catfish, crawfish étouffée, and pastry-clad po-boy shrimp. Though a bottle of most vintages on the list can set your budget back, wine is also available by the glass. *Tip:* Try to snag a table near the window wall at the back.

Candlestick Inn (127 Taney Street; 417/334-3633) is a Branson institution where locals go to celebrate birthdays and anniversaries Food leans toward the Creole and Cajun, with the likes of crabcakes, but you'll also find Long Island duckling and veal dishes on the menu. Fresh seafood and aged Angus beef are considered the house specialties. Perched atop Mount Branson, the restaurant overlooks the town, with the view at its best on a clear night during the holiday season when myriad lights twinkle below. In summer, get a table on the deck. To get to Candlestick Inn, take Missouri Highway 76 east and drive uphill. The restaurant's sign is about halfway up on the left.

A LITTLE LUXURY

An expensive dinner for two in Paris or San Francisco can cost $400 or more. In Branson, expect to spend about $100 when you're pulling out all the stops. To be truthful, even then you won't find many places that serve truly gourmet food. What you will find in the best of the area's relatively upscale restaurants are meals that are more carefully prepared and are served in attractive environments.

Devil's Pool (Big Cedar Lodge Resort at 612 Devil's Pool

Road, Ridgedale; 417/335-5141) has an ambience that would make the restaurant special whatever its location. A huge stone fireplace warms the dining room whenever there's a chill in the air, and lights from hand-wrought chandeliers cast a glow over the rustic, yet elegant, room with its antique furnishings and hundred-year-old mahogany bar. In case you are an animal lover and offended by the mounted animal heads on the wall, you'll be happy to know there's outdoor balcony seating when weather permits. Considered the region's finest restaurant, Devil's Pool specialties include hickory-smoked prime rib and praline rainbow trout.

For more casual and less expensive dining at Big Cedar Lodge, **Top of the Rock** is housed in what was formerly a private residence. Built of native stone, timbers, and hand-wrought metal railings, the structure blends perfectly with its outdoor environment. Menu offerings include house-made pasta, rotisserie chicken, pizza, seafood, grilled pork, salads, sandwiches, and specialty coffee. Seating choices are either indoors or on an outdoor terrace high above Table Rock Lake.

Chateau Grille (Chateau at the Lake, 415 North Highway 265; 417/334-1161), another restaurant overlooking Table Rock Lake, is one of only four in the state of Missouri that has been awarded four diamonds by the AAA. Decor is posh, with thick carpets and cherry paneling. The view is panoramic. The food runs the gastronomic gamut from smoked scallops and sorghum-glazed salmon to pecan-seared rack of lamb and veal tenderloin with pan-seared foie gras. Among the scrumptious desserts is the pecan torte with chocolate-caramel sauce.

Buckingham's Restaurant and Oasis (Palace Inn at 2800 West Highway 76; 417/337-7777) seems downright pretentious when compared to its Branson neighbors. First of all, there's the safari-meets-south-seas decor that looks somewhat like a stage set, with palm trees, faux animal skins, and exotic birds in the hand-painted murals. Then there are the culinary offerings such as ostrich tenderloin, venison medallions, and quail. Less unusual menu choices include prime rib, smoked pork, and steak. The restaurant is open for lunch and dinner. Reservations are advised.

Though entrées at Dimitri's Casual Gourmet Dining (500

East Main Street; 417/334-0888) can run as high as $44.99 for lobster tail, it's a puzzle as to who would order lobster in Middle America when the catfish are local, fresh, and cost $19.95. In fact, most of the entrées at Dimitri's—like chicken Française, prime rib, shish kebab, and trout amandine (all served with salad and potatoes or spaghetti) fall into the $16 to $22 range. Appetizers include a few traditional Greek offerings such as spanakopita (cheese-spinach pie, $5.99) and stuffed grape leaves ($6.99). Desserts are spendy by Branson standards, and most of them are flamed.

SWEET TALK

Sometimes the need for dessert becomes so compelling that nothing will do but finding a pastry shop or ice cream parlor. Fortunately, desserts are an important part of the Branson culinary lineup—so much so that some eateries noted for their desserts offer very little else except the beverages that enhance the sweet things.

Cakes 'n' Cream Dessert Parlor (2805 West Highway 76; 417/334-4929) is the place to go when you're hungering for a piece of strawberry shortcake. Sit at the **Engler Block's sidewalk café** and savor one of the cobblers with blackberry, blueberry, raspberry, gooseberry, elderberry, strawberry, apple, or peach filling. And when you cast the thought of calories to the wind, go for the Ozark Hot Fudge Turtle (butter pecan ice cream with hot fudge caramel pecan topping, whipped cream, and maraschino cherry) at **Delicious Delights** (2925 West Highway 76; 417/335-3500).

THE CHAIN GANG

For readers who are loyal to their favorite chain restaurants even when they're on vacation, the following list reveals their Branson locations:

A & W	300 Tanger Blvd.	417/337-7112
Applebee's	1836 W. Highway 76	417/336-5053
Blimpie	4017 W. Highway 76	417/339-4642

Burger King	1026 W. Main	417/334-2468
Country Kitchen	3225 W. Highway 76	417/334-2766
Dairy Queen	2620 W. Highway 76	417/335-8974
Domino's Pizza	Junction Highways 76 and 165	417/335-6789
Hardee's	W. Highway 76	417/334-1121
Kentucky Fried Chicken (KFC)	1550 Highway 248	417/339-3610
McDonald's	2214 W. Highway 76	417/335-2505
	Highway 248 and Epps Road	417/337-7744
	2050 W. Highway 76	417/335-5768
	3525 W. Highway 76	417/339-4218
	515 W. Main St.	417/335-4909
McGuffey's Eclectic Eatery	2600 W. Highway 76	417/336-3600
	Highway 248	417/335-8680
Olive Garden	3790 W. Highway 76	417/337-5811
Outback	1910 W. Highway 76	417/334-6306
Red Lobster	3559 Shepherd of the Hills	417/337-5988
Shoney's	1950 W. Highway 76	417/335-6855
Subway	607 S. Highway 165	417/336-2823
	1314 W. Highway 76	417/334-7827
	1494 Highway 248	417/336-4418
Taco Bell	Shepherd of the Hills	417/335-5394
	2000 W. Highway 76	417/335-2576
Wendy's	510 W. Highway 76	417/334-1941

ALTERNATIVE DINING OPTIONS

Even when restaurant meals are relatively inexpensive, as they are in Branson, the cost of eating out can become significant. There are, however, several ways you can contain food costs without sacrificing quality or enjoyment.

When you're traveling by car, that all-important ice chest can serve as a mini refrigerator and save dozens of dollars even during the course of a three- or four-day stay. If your car

Tricks on Buying Treats

Vacation's the time when we treat ourselves to the snacks, desserts, and beverages we try to limit when we're at home. But as you know, single cans of soda purchased at a theme park or other attraction and from hotel vending machines may cost almost half of what a twelve-can carton sells for at the supermarket. Tiny bags of chips, pretzels, and trail mix at convenience stores go for the same price as much larger bags of the identical snack do elsewhere. And fancy desserts can cost more than a regular meal.

Making a supermarket sweep at the beginning of your stay can help solve the dollar-here-five-dollars-there drain on your vacation budget. Put soft drinks and bottled water in your shopping cart. Buy the larger-sized bags of chips and transfer to snack-sized servings in plastic bags you've brought from home. As far as desserts are concerned, you'll find coupons such as "complimentary dessert when an entrée is ordered" and "buy one ice cream cone, get the second one free" in brochure racks, entertainment publications, and newspapers.

is a rental, consider buying an inexpensive Styrofoam chest at one of the discount stores.

Take advantage of complimentary continental breakfasts when they are included in the cost of your room—even if you're not a breakfast eater. Even though signs request that people don't take any food out of the dining room, help yourself to a piece of fruit, a bagel, a sweet roll, or a container of yogurt from the serving table to eat later in the day. After all, the cost of the food was factored in when the hotel's or motel's room rates were determined. If you eat in the breakfast room, however, it's not considered cricket to take more food with you.

A WEEK'S WORTH OF PICNIC POSSIBILITIES

Although Branson restaurant fare is not always interesting, the area's picnic sites are. Paired with food bought at one of area supermarkets, sandwich shops, and delicatessens, this *al fresco* dining can produce memorable mealtimes. Here are some suggestions:

1. Have a salad lunch or supper at the Indian Point picnic area at the south end of the Indian Point peninsula. Buy a selection—coleslaw, three-bean, pasta, and chicken salad— at **Country Mart's** (1447 Highway 248; 417/334-6461) deli counter, plus a loaf of French bread and maybe a bottle of wine.

2. Get a pan-style pizza with sausage and homemade tomato sauce to take out from **Mr. G's Chicago Style Pizza** (202 North Commercial Street; 417/335-8156) or a California Pizza (chicken, artichoke hearts, roasted red peppers, and marinated Roma tomatoes) from **Luigi's Pizza Kitchen** (Cedar Ridge Center, 14475 Highway 248; 417/339-4544) for a gratifying lunch at Stockstill Park (off James F. Epps Road).

3. Order sandwiches from **Schlotzsky's Deli** (1946 West Highway 76; 417/334-5274) to eat while you're sitting on a dock bench overlooking Lake Taneycomo at North Beach Park. You might want to try the Original (ham, salami, cotto salami, mozzarella, Parmesan, cheddar, mustard, chopped black olives, onions, lettuce, and tomato on toasted sourdough bun; $3.39, small; $4.39 regular includes chips and beverage).

4. Pull up to **Tran's** drive-through window (see Scouting the Buffets, above) for Chinese food to eat at Table Rock State Park. Buy enough for three people and you'll probably have more than enough for six.

5. Buy submarine foot-long sandwiches with a variety of fillings at **Subway** (see addresses above). Cut each sandwich in as many pieces as there are members of your group. Then share them, along with cookies and beverages from the supermarket, at a table overlooking Table Rock Lake at the Dewey Short Information Center.

6. Patronize the take-out window of your favorite drive-in (this may take a while if there are several people with dif-

ferent favorites in your party). Take your sacks to the over-look at the Ruth and Paul Henning Conservation Area (off West Highway 76 about a mile west of Shepherd of the Hills), where you can sit on the wide stone wall and gaze at the view while you eat. Walk off your lunch by taking one of the area's hiking trails or strolling along the path that follows the overlook's walls. Outdoor displays at intervals along the path visually educate visitors as to the area's geology, plants, and animal life.

7. Start the day with a breakfast picnic. Go to **Tom's Town Bakery** (120 Commercial Street; 417/239-1892) and buy some delicious cinnamon rolls, doughnuts, and chocolate bars. Add some fresh fruit or juice and take your meal to Old School Park (near the intersection of Berry Road and West Highway 76).

Branson Dining Tips

Here are some tips on Branson dining that may help you plan your mealtime choices:

- A moderately priced meal costs no more than $10. A meal is considered expensive when it costs more than $10, and very pricey when the entrée tops $20.

- Eating your big meal in the middle of the day usually saves money. In many restaurants, entrées on lunch menus cost less than those at dinner—even when they're the same. And though you can eat just as much food, midday buffet prices are often lower than thy are in the evening.

- Since Branson is tour bus heaven and people on tours usually are taken to the bigger buffets, it's best to avoid these restaurants between 11:30 A.M. and 1 P.M. and from 5 to 7 P.M.

- Some restaurants serve beer. Some serve only wine. Others serve no alcoholic beverages. If your mealtime happiness depends on having a drink, you'd better phone ahead to the restaurant you're considering.

- Most restaurants are open daily, but hours can vary with the season. It's a good idea to call ahead if you're uncertain.

When you know in advance that you will be eating a number of picnic meals, pack items such as a spatula, steak knife, barbecue fork, and padded glove in your luggage, adding variety to your menu choices. Certainly, it takes time to get a fire going, but the parks and other picnic sites equipped with grills are almost always pleasant places to spend an hour or two—and some of them are spectacular.

4

Getting Around

About 83 percent of its visitors travel to Branson by automobile, motor home, or other personal vehicles. And although Missouri's country music capital is perceived as a mecca for bus tours, only about 7 percent of its visitors are members of organized tours. The remaining 10 percent arrive by commercial and charter airline flights or by private plane.

The commercial and charter air passengers deplane at **Branson/Springfield Regional Airport.** Unless they are met at the airport by representatives of group tours that originate in the area, these travelers have a trio of options as to how they will get to Branson.

Many of them rent cars, usually in advance of arrival. This is usually the most practical and economical transportation for families, since it will allow them to drive where they wish during their stay for the rental fee plus the cost of gasoline. It's also the most convenient for people who want to visit multiple attractions, take in some shows, and engage in outdoor activities such as golf, hiking, and boating.

Among the national rental agencies located at the airport or at off-premise sites nearby are:

Avis Rent A Car	800/831-2847 or 417/864-4466
Budget Car Rental	800/527-0700 or 417/831-2662
Enterprise Rent-A-Car	800/325-8007 or 417/866-0300

Hertz Rent A Car	800/654-3131 or 417/865-1681
National Car Rental	800/CAR-RENT or 417/865-5311
Sears Car Rental	800-527/0770 or 417/831-0661
Thrifty Car Rental	800/367-2277 or 417/866-8777

Some of the Springfield agencies include:

Martin Rental & Leasing	417/862-8522
Practical Rent-A-Car	417/863-7368
Priceless Car Rental	417/886-3884

Gray Line offers portal-to-portal shuttle service from the airport to Branson. Shuttles depart from the airport at 10 and 11:30 A.M., 2:30, 4:40, and 9:30 P.M. The fare is $30 per person one way ($55 round trip), and reservations must be made to assure service (reservations may be canceled up to twenty-four hours prior to arrival without penalty). Reservations may be made online at www.bransongrayline.com/shuttles.html or by phoning 800/542-6768 or 417/334-8687. It's also possible to hire taxis at the airport. When you're traveling with three or more people in your party, you may find that this is your most inexpensive way of getting to and from the airport.

DRIVER'S EDUCATION

If you're arriving by automobile, you'll find that Branson is easy to get to—most visitors use U.S. Highway 65, which runs north and south. Once you're there, however, you'll discover that, like most places where a lot goes on within a relatively small area, Branson suffers from monumental traffic jams. And although millions of dollars were spent on the little city's infrastructure during the 1990s, problems persist. This is partly because tourism has increased so dramatically during this period, and also because more and more theaters, attractions, lodging places, and shopping malls have been constructed along Missouri Highway 76 (also known as 76 Country Boulevard and the Strip). Before showtimes when traffic is heavy, it can take as long as two hours to get from one end of the theater-lined thoroughfare to the other.

Therefore, if you don't have one already, it's a good idea to get a map that indicates the locations of the various theaters *before* you plan to do any serious driving. That way, you can devise alternate routes to the shows you want to see and the attractions you want to visit. Branson is changing so rapidly that it's important to get the latest map available. You'll have the best chance of doing that at the **Branson Chamber of Commerce Visitors Center** (269 Highway 248; 800/214-3661 or 417/334-4136; just west of the Highway 65 overpass at the Highway 248 interchange one junction north of Highway 76). The Welcome Center is open Monday through Saturday from 8 A.M. to 5 P.M., and on Sunday from 10 A.M. to 4 P.M. Hours are extended during peak season.

The best Branson maps are color-coded, indicating two east–west roads north of Missouri Highway 76—Shepherd of the Hills Expressway (red) and Gretna Road–Roark Valley Road (blue)—and one east–west road, Green Mountain Drive (yellow), south of the highway. Taking these roads in combination with the several north–south streets connecting them can save you hours of travel time during the average visitors' stay of three to four days.

Additional theaters, hotels, and attractions that front on Shepherd of the Hills Expressway (Missouri Highway 165) can be accessed by alternate routes, too. The other tourist area in Branson is downtown, which is on Main Street—the part of Missouri Highway 76 that's east of U.S. Highway 65.

Before you go out on your initial drive around town, use a highlighter to mark the principal streets you'll be using during your Branson stay. If at all possible, I like to take my familiarization drive in any new place early in the morning before most drivers are out and about. That way I can get the lay of the land without having to think too much about traffic. Since I often travel alone and won't have someone in the passenger seat to tell me where to turn, I try to memorize landmarks on that first drive. Knowing that there's a Wendy's or an Amoco station or a Wal-Mart on the corner just before my destination makes it easier for me to navigate. When you're traveling with a family, it's a good idea for the person who will be doing the most driving to go solo on his or her first tour around town.

That way there will be no distractions while the driver concentrates on getting the lay of the land.

Some of the basic shortcut strategies we've discovered in Branson follow. (In addition, you'll find tips on the easiest routes to several of the theaters in chapter 8, Showtime.)

- To get from the south side of the street on the east end of West Missouri Highway 76 to an attraction on the western reaches of the highway, take the nearest north–south street that can be accessed by making right-hand turns to Green Mountain Drive. Take Green Mountain to the north–south street before the attraction and turn left if it's located on the north side of the street. Take the north–south street beyond and turn right if the attraction is on the south side.

- To get from the north side/east end of West Highway 76 going west, take the nearest north–south street that can be accessed by making a right-hand turn off Highway 76. Drive to Roark Road and turn left. Turn left again when you get to the first north–south street before your destination for an attraction on the north side of Highway 76 and turn right. Drive to the north–south street beyond and turn left for locations on the south side of the highway.

- If your location is on the north side of the street at the east part of West Highway 76 and your destination is on the Strip to the west, take the nearest north–south street you can access with a right-hand turn. Drive to Gretna Road/Roark Road. Take Gretna Road/Roark Road to the north–south street before your destination and make a left-hand turn if it's on the south side of the street; drive to the street beyond your destination and turn right if it's north side of the street.

- When your location is on the south side of the street on the east portion of West Highway 76, to get to destinations in the west, take the nearest north–south road to the north–south connecting road before your destination and turn right if it's on the south side; take the north–south street beyond your destination and turn left if it's on the north side.

- Pat Nash Road, which runs east–west, can be used in conjunction with Gretna Road for easier access to attractions between its east end and Shepherd of the Hills Expressway.

- During periods of heavy traffic, access to attractions on Shepherd of the Hills Expressway is easiest when made via Roark Road.

Branson's **Travel & Recreation Information Program (TRIP),** mentioned briefly in chapter 1, can also help you navigate more efficiently around town. Five main components make up the TRIP system:

1. A Web site (www.branson.tripusa.com) can be used before you leave home to get travel tips as well as browse through a list of area activities and lodgings.

2. A radio network (tune to 1610 AM) lets you know where the traffic is flowing freely and where it isn't.

3. Electronic message boards are located wherever conditions warrant, flashing important messages regarding accidents and road construction.

4. Kiosks provide interactive displays that feature touch screens providing information—including weather forecasts and routes to destinations out of town. You can also purchase Internet time at some of the kiosks so that you can retrieve your e-mail and conduct other business.

5. A phone-in information line (417/336-0439 or 877/4-TRIP) gives up-to-the-minute, easy-to-follow instructions and phone-in line coordinates with Branson's official city map, which you can pick up at city hall (110 West Maddux Street; 417/334-3345). The information is available twenty-four hours a day and is free.

If you have arrived in Branson without transportation and decide you want to rent a car, the following are local rental agencies to contact:

A-1 Auto Rental
819 Highway 165 South
Branson, MO 65616
800/335-2932

Enterprise Rent-A-Car
HCR 9, Box 1180-B
Branson, MO 65616
417/338-2280

Rent-A-Wreck
986 East Highway 76
Branson, MO 65616
888/761-7724

Getting around in Branson without a car may be a snap for solo travelers and couples who like to hike long distances. For most families—especially for those with small children—it's more complicated. Still, taxis and trolleys ply the main tourist routes and shuttles run from various hotels and motels to the theme parks, theaters, shopping centers, and other attractions (phone A-OK Shuttles and Tours, 417/334-8687, for schedules). Shuttles cost $5 per person one way and $8 round trip. When you take a taxi, do remember to tell the driver you want to go by the fastest route. The shortest route often takes longer and therefore costs more.

Sight-Seeing from Different Perspectives

Gray Line (1316 West Highway 76, Suite 192; 877/900-8687 or 417/334-5463; www.bransongrayline.com) offers guided tours of Branson and the Ozarks. Among them is a three-hour tour in November and December during the Festival of Lights, which passes by all the major illuminations. Another, offered only on Wednesdays at 9 A.M., is called the Antique and Craft Road Show (see chapter 11, Day Trips).

Dome cars with panoramic views offer passengers on the **Branson Scenic Railway's Ozark Zephyr** (201 East Main Street; 800/2-TRAIN-2 or 417/334-6110) a chance to see the Ozarks in all their glory without having to contend with traffic. The southbound journey on the railway's 1940s and 1950s rolling stock begins in downtown Branson and takes you over the Lake Taneycomo Dam and into the north Arkansas Ozarks. The northbound excursion goes to the James River and across the Roark Canyon trestle. The railroad is busiest in October, when the bubble glass provides great fall foliage viewing. At any time of year, you'll go through tunnels and travel along streams tumbling over the rocks. Each round trip is about forty miles and lasts about an hour and forty-five minutes. Snacks are available; there's also a dinner train excursion.

You can go sight-seeing, too, by **"Riding the Duck"** (2320 Highway 76 next to Wal-Mart; 417/334-DUCK). The Ducks (technically they're DUKWs) are surplus amphibious landing craft that were developed for use by the U.S. Army in World War II. Passengers ride in the amphibians down 76 Country Boulevard, across Table Rock Dam, and splash right into Table Rock Lake. During the eighty-minute trip, the Ducks pass by several of the area's points of interest, including Shepherd of the Hills Fish Hatchery. They also climb up to the top of Baird Mountain, the highest point in the Branson region, where the views of Table Rock Lake are spectacular. Adults pay $14.95, children $7.50, for this adventure.

Exploring the waters around Branson is a snap when you take one of the commercial boat cruises (see chapter 6, Attractions). If you're more adventurous, you may want to rent some sort of watercraft. Pontoons, motorboats, canoes, kayaks, and sailboats are available. To get an eagle's-eye view—at a fairly high price as well—you might take a **Table Rock Helicopter** flight (3309 Highway 76; 417/334-6102; www.tablerockhelicopters.com) or a balloon flight with Ozark Balloon Port (2235 Smyrna Road, Ozark; 417/581-7373). The company has several sites in the area from which they launch the balloons, which are in the air for about an hour and a half during a typical flight. The cost is about $180 per person.

5

Shopping and Souvenirs

DISCOUNT OUTLETS

Not too long ago, when Branson residents had serious shopping to do, most of them went someplace else—to Springfield, perhaps, or Kansas City. But not anymore. The escalation in tourism has been matched by a proliferation of shopping opportunities: from large discount malls and boutiques to studios where you can buy one-of-a-kind crafts made by local artisans. Though a dismaying number of gift and souvenir stores have sprung up during the past decade (single owners have several stores with different names but virtually the same merchandise in various locations), you can find treasures worth buying if you take the time to seek them out.

The largest outlet mall, **Factory Merchants of Branson** (1000 Pat Nash Drive; 417/335-6686), is a two-story complex with canopied walkways. Also referred to as Red Roof Mall, it contains more than ninety stores, which advertise savings of from 25 to 70 percent. It's a good place to shop for children's clothing, since **Buster Brown Kidswear, Bugle Boy,** and **Carter's Childrenswear** are among the discount stores. People in the market for homeware can check out **Lenox, Pfaltzgraff, Kitchen Collection, Corning/Revere,** and **Chicago Cutlery.** Clothing outlets include **Izod, Hush Puppies, Van Heusen,** and **Florsheim.** Among the discount coupons available are $10

off a $50 purchase from Hush Puppies, ten percent off a pur-
chase of $30 or more at Lenox, 30 percent off one item at Pfalt-
zgraff, and $5 off a $30 ($10 off a $60) purchase at Kitchen
Collection. To make efficient use of your shopping time, stop
at the mall office for a map and shopping guide before you
begin to browse.

Carolina Mills Factory Outlet (3615 West Highway 76;
417/3334-2291) was Branson's first factory outlet, opening in
1975. Housed in an immense warehouselike space, it's a bargain heaven for people who sew, with bolt upon bolt of uphol-
stery fabric and card after card of discounted lace. You can
buy finished goods, too—everything from sheets and towels to
Levis and square-dance dresses. Prices, however, seem generally higher than they ought to be. The real bargains can be
found in the "$5 Room," where all items cost five dollars or
less. Even then, you'll have to be discriminating (seasonal
items like Christmas ties and woven Hallowe'en place mats are
among the best deals). Coupons for free Branson hats when
making a $10 purchase are widely distributed. Unless you
really like what you're buying, however, it's not worth the purchase simply to get a free hat.

Factory Shoppes at Branson Meadows (4562 Gretna
Road; 417/339-2580) are Victorian-style buildings containing
about four dozen outlets and an eleven-screen movie theater.
Since the films are first run, nonshoppers might want to catch
a flick while their companions are checking out the merchandise at the thirty-thusand-square-foot **VF** (Vanity Fair, **Jan-
Sport, Jantzen, Healthtex, Wrangler, Lee,** and other brands
conglomerate). Prices at VF are one-half off the lowest ticketed price. A coupon for an additional 10 percent off a $100
purchase is available in VF brochures, which you'll find all
around town. Other outlets among the factory shops include
Casual Male Big & Tall, Golf USA, and **Farberware.** Hungry
and you've spent all your money? **Mountain Man Nut & Fruit
Company** offers free daily samples. **Factory Shoppes** put out
their own coupon book, which is free upon presentation of
a coupon found in *TravelHost* brochures. In addition, among
coupons issued by individual stores are one from Big & Tall
that offers 20 percent off on the purchase of one item.

At the **Tanger Outlet Center** (300 Tanger Boulevard; 417/337-2580), more than five dozen manufacturers' outlet stores are located on one level. Since the parking lot is large, you can save steps by driving around the stores' periphery before you park to locate the shops you want to visit. The shops include **Create A Stuffed Animal, Music for a Song, Camp Coleman, Vitamin World, Reebok** (look for their $10 off a $75 purchase offer), **Samsonite, Guess, Stone Mountain Handbags, The Icing, Tommy Hilfiger, OshKosh B'Gosh, Polo Ralph Lauren, Ann Taylor Loft,** and **Arnold Palmer Golf Store.** Tanger Mall puts out a free coupon book, available at several of its stores and at the mall office.

Most outlet mall hours are from 9 A.M. to 9 P.M. Monday through Saturday, and Sunday from 10 A.M. to 7 P.M., with abbreviated hours in winter.

HIGHWAY 76 STRIP MALLS

All along Highway 76, tucked between the theaters, are strip malls—groups of various businesses like you find in any population center. The following paragraphs highlight the shops in these malls that we found most interesting. You may have other favorites. The best way to determine that is by checking them out.

Branson Heights Shopping Center (1557 Highway 76) is the location of **Quilts & Quilts Country Store** (417/334-3243), with one of the biggest selections of quilting supplies in the area. The center is also the locale of the **Branson Heights Flea Market**, a neat place to poke about if your passion is collectibles.

Branson Mall (2206 Highway 76) is the place to go if you're looking for tacky hillbilly gifts (at **Hicks From the Sticks**; 417/334-2017). It's also home to the biggest supermarket in town, **Nowell's**—a great place to shop for snacks, soft drinks, and such at reasonable prices (be sure to check the racks at Nowell's front entrance for brochures and discount coupons—there's one in *TravelHost* for a free Branson Mall coupon book).

If I could shop at only one Branson mall, I would definitely choose **Grand Village** (2800 Highway 76: 417/336-SHOP). It's several steps above the usual strip mall as far as ambience is concerned, with flower beds and plants in pots, storybook buildings, and lots of trees and benches. Among its most unusual shops is **Reigning Cats & Dogs** (417/336-7212), carrying items for both pets and their owners. **Queen Anne's Lace** contains an ethereal array of curtains, table toppers, mantel scarfs, and runners, and **Peter Engler Design** (417/335-6862) features works by Branson's best known wood-carver.

Most impressive of the twenty-six shops in the complex, **Kringles** (417/336-7246), the largest year-round Christmas store in Missouri, consists of six galleries. The stars at Kringles Collectibles are the Santas and nutcrackers; Kringles Glass and Kringles Ornaments focus on thousands of tree decorations from around the world. Kringles Village Collection and Kringles Keepsakes provide holiday magic galore in the form of miniature snow-sprinkled villages—the Snow, Dickens, and North Pole Villages are especially enchanting. The most delightful of the galleries, to my mind, is Frosty's, where thousands of snowmen peer from shelves, ceiling, counters, and corners. Snow even falls year-round outside the shop's windows.

Among Grand Village coupons is one for $5 off on a $25 purchase at any of the center's shops.

OFF-STRIP STRIP MALLS

You may find more of the locals patronizing some of these shopping centers, but that doesn't mean they're without one or two interesting places to spend your money.

Cedar Ridge Plaza (1447 Highway 248) is where you'll find the local **Kmart** (**Wal-Mart** is at Branson Mall). There's also a good grocery store called **Country Mart** (417/334-6461) as well as the **Wine Company** (417/334-4551).

At the **Falls Center** (3265 Falls Parkway; 417/343-3400), **Elegant Illusions** (417/336-4882) specializes in faux jewels—baubles, bangles, and such designed to look like the real thing. **Dressin' Gaudy** (417/336-3465) carries clothes that are about as wild as they get in Branson. **Fabulous Fakes** (417/336-2983)

at the **IMAX Entertainment Complex** (3562 Shepherd of the Hills Expressway; 417/-336-2983)
is another place to buy ersatz jewelry.

The Marketplace (417/881-0600) consists of a small group of shops, and since it's right next to the Welk Resort Center on Missouri Highway 165, it's a place to browse if you've arrived early for the show in order to get a good parking place.

Victorian Village Shops (3044 Shepherd of the Hills Expressway; 417/334-6625) include **Gingerbread Kids** (417/335-7900), which carries educational toys as well as youngsters' clothing; **Heirloom Lace** (417/334-7048), another good place to shop for lace curtains, and **Leather Etc.** (417/336-4333), where handcrafted leather goods by Glenn Haworth are made and sold.

SPECIALTY SHOPS

You'll be missing a great deal—and some great deals—if you confine your shopping to the discount outlets and strip malls. Some of the area's most interesting shops are concentrated in the older downtown area or scattered here and there around Branson.

Downtown Branson has some unusual businesses that dedicated shoppers won't want to miss. The "must-see" downtown store, **Dick's Oldtime 5 & 10** (103 West Main Street; 417/334-2410), holds some fifty thousand different items. Crammed floor to ceiling, it's the repository for jacks, hula hoops, and jump ropes; ceramic fish bookends and old-time "kit-kat" clocks; Blue Waltz perfume and fishing weights; calendars and motor oil. Look up, down, and around to see tulip bulbs and rubber spiders, silver doilies, sun catchers, paper dolls, kaleidoscopes, gliders, scrub boards, and necco wafers.

The Guitar Shop (704 South Commercial Street; 417/334-3030) is the place to go when you're hankering for a dulcimer or mandolin, for it specializes in vintage and used string instruments. If you're in town for a few days, you might arrange to take a couple of guitar lessons there, too.

Lefty Lane & Gifts (104 North Commercial Street; 417/336-3920) specializes in practical items—left-handed scissors, can openers, knives, mugs, and dozens of other articles—that make life a little easier for people who are left-handed. There are ego-boosters, too, such as T-shirts and bumper stickers that proclaim the virtues of being lefties.

Orphanage Dolls (111 West Main Street; 417/34-2900) may be the Branson shopping highlight for doll lovers. Lots of Raggedy Anns and Raggedy Andies; scads of Barbies, ethnic, and storybook dolls are on display, as are multiple Kewpies and Madame Alexanders. There's a Shirley Temple doll, too, in its original box ($900). **Mar-Lea's Boutique** (114 West Main Street; 417/334-5445) carries fancy clothes, decorated with sequins, spangles, and beads, for grown-up dolls who dress to be seen.

The **Engler Block** (1335 West Highway 76; 417/335-2200) contains a number of independent shopkeepers. It is, to my way of thinking, one of the best shopping spots within the Branson city limits. The building, formerly a factory warehouse, has been converted into a crafts mall—with crafts supplies, instructions, and finished products for sale. More than a dozen shops feature a variety of crafts that range from pottery and leather work to puppets and wood carvings.

You'll be greeted at the doorway of **Santa's Workshop** by the fourteen-foot *Woodcarver Santa.* Crafted by owner Jesse Kuh, the piece was carved from a single basswood log. Carved walking sticks, pig pokes, cattle sorters, and the other objects for sale aren't cheap, but offer lots of value for the money you spend on them.

At **Morning Glory Glassworks** (417/334-0564), ready-made stained-glass windows and sun catchers sparkle in jewel-like colors. **Play in Clay Pottery** (417/239-1127) features hand-thrown pottery by owners John and Pamela Hagen, as well as by other well-known Ozark potters. Incidentally, the puppet shop is called **Mastercraft Puppets 'n More** (417/337-5100).

The most amazing shop in the block is not connected to the others and isn't that of a craftsperson. It's called **Unique Impressions** (1335 West Highway 76; 417/335-4817) and contains an incredible supply of rubber stamps—more than sixty thousand of them, as well as stamp pads in a rainbow of colors, brass stencils, and scrapbooking supplies. Catalogs from seven different rubber stamp companies are also for sale in the thirty-four-hundred-square-foot store.

The Flagstore (1318 West Highway 76; 417/334-1776) underscores one of Branson's themes—patriotism. More than two million of Branson's annual visitors are veterans. Annual events include Veterans Day and Independence Day celebrations. So there's a lot of flag waving going on. At the Flagstore, you'll find historical flags, flagpoles from 12 to 120 feet high, patriotic bumper stickers and other items. Flags of other nations are for sale, too—useful if you want to celebrate your ethnic heritage at Silver Dollar City's annual International Festival. There are wind socks, too, in the form of witches, a slicker-clad duck with a frog in his pocket, and a cat in red overalls.

Log Cabin Quilts (3612 Shepherd of the Hills Expressway; 417/335-4236) is, in my opinion, the best of the shops that specialize in handmade quilts. Patterns for the quilts and their fabrics are both designer and traditional, but all of them—as well as the quilted pillow shams, vests, jackets, bags, Christmas tree skirts, and wall hangings—are imported. They're hand stitched in the Far East, primarily in India and China. Especially handsome are the quilts in the wedding ring pattern with crocheted medallions in the set-together (the plain fabric sections of a quilt where the various blocks are attached). The Log Cabin's quilts range in price from $59.95 to $700. A coupon that's widely distributed offers $5 off sale-priced quilt purchases.

The **Butterfly Place gift shop** (2400 Highway 165; 417/332-2231) focuses on—you guessed it—butterflies. Whether you're looking for hair decorations, garden ornaments, scarves, or dessert plates, you'll find butterflies made of sequins, clay, brass, chiffon, and stained glass. There are drinking glasses and coffee mugs, thousand- and fifteen-hundred-piece jigsaw puzzles, even removable butterfly tattoos.

Foozles (4540 North Gretna Road; 417/339-2424) is great for rainy-day browsing. Along with a large selection of travel guides, it also carries a lot of children's books. The store's specialty is discounted books, so you'll want to spend some time checking out the bargain tables where you can find reading material that costs one-fourth of its original price.

The very best place to find quality crafts is at **Silver Dollar City** (see chapter 11, Day Trips). Among the permanent crafters who make and sell their wares on site are jewelry makers, glassblowers, tole painters, leather workers, wood-carvers, calligraphers, dried flower arrangers, and potters. Others make lye soap, knives, dolls, baskets, and dulcimers. During the annual crafts festivals, the number of artisans swells to about 175, adding dozens more places that produce one-of-a-kind items.

ANTIQUES, ANYONE?

There are people who visit Branson and never see a show, don't go near the water. They have only one mission in mind—to scour the area for antiques. If you're interested in articles from the past, the following are among your best bets for finding them in Branson. If you're passionate about collecting, however, you'll also want to head for the little town of Ozark, about midway between Branson and Springfield (see chapter 11, Day Trips).

The Apple Tree Mall (1830 Highway 76; 417/335-2133), formerly a supermarket, has been converted into more than four hundred stalls, whose tenants have a wide variety of items for sale. You'll find homemade jam next to depression glass; rock paintings across the aisle from hand-crocheted doilies. Great fun if you've loads of time.

Cadwell's Downtown Flea Market (114 East Main Street; 417/334-5051) has been around Branson since the early 1980s. Though items are generally priced at close to their actual market value (and above), if you're knowledgeable, you'll occasionally find a great buy.

Coffelt Country Flea Market (675 Highway 165; 417/334-7611) was once part of the Coffelt family farm. Designed to look like a hillbilly town in the Ozarks, it contains about three dozen shops. **Quilt Connection** (417/334-6523), the **Backward Seed** (herbs and homemade soap; 417/339-1700), and shops

Branson Photo Ops

When photo albums play an important part in your post-trip pleasure, the following suggestions will give you some ideas for picture-perfect settings:

- If your group plans to take a ride in one of the horse-drawn carriages that ply the Taneycomo lakefront downtown, have everyone strike a pose before taking off. The carriages are especially popular with wedding parties and on prom nights, so Saturday nights in spring and warm-weather afternoons are ideal times to take photos if you need models and don't have a friend handy.

- Almost all of the craftspeople and storytellers at Silver Dollar City are willing subjects for pictures (see chapter 11, Day Trips).

- Catch the *Showboat Branson Belle* as she leaves or comes in to the dock on Table Rock Lake.

- Though video recorders are prohibited at the shows, regular photos are permitted. If you're serious about taking pictures, be sure you're sitting near the front.

- Drive south of Branson about two miles on U.S. Highway 65 to the junction with Missouri Highway 165. Turn right and drive west about three miles to the scenic overlook (it's marked by a sign, but you'll know you're there anyway). The knock-your-socks-off view encompasses all of Branson. Use a telephoto as well as a wide-angle lens, if you have them.

- **The Old Time Photo & Tin Types** (1335 West Highway 76; 417/335-2563), **Aunt B's Old Time Photos** (2855 West Highway 76; 417/336-9876), and **Moe's Old Time Photos** (116 West Main Street; 417/334-2004) are just three of the places in town where you can pose in costume for photos. Backdrops vary from saloons and dance halls to formal sitting rooms. Costumes are mostly in western, pioneer, and Victorian styles.

where you can buy everything from rag rugs to rag dolls make this a popular, but sometimes crowded, browsing territory.

In Branson's sister city, Hollister—about two miles away—you'll find a couple of other antiques treasure troves. **Green Lantern Antiques** (15 Downing Street, Hollister; 417/334-7541) is small, cluttered, and great for people with lots of perseverance (be sure to look up, down, and in boxes). Down the street, **Flea Collar Antique Mall** (1 Downing Street, Hollister; 417/335-4056) is perhaps the most interesting antiques shop in the Branson-Hollister environs. On the first and third Saturday of each month at 6:30 P.M., the Flea Collar is the venue for estate and antiques auctions—great events for serious collectors and people who like that kind of free entertainment.

AMONG YOUR SOUVENIRS

The best souvenirs are those you keep using or looking at long after the trip is only a memory. Among favorite Branson keepsakes are tapes, CDs, and videos that visitors purchase of their favorite shows. Of course, you'll find the standard mementos in Branson, too, perhaps in greater abundance than at most vacation spots. T-shirts, caps, coffee mugs, and tote bags are only a few of the items you'll find. And if you're determined to get a souvenir you'll have forever, you might want to have a Branson tattoo.

6

Attractions

Although its country music shows have catapulted Branson to touristic fame, the town was originally a resort area, and its first shows were considered simply an added attraction to its hills and lakes. As shows have come to dominate Branson's center stage, other attractions have been—and are being—added at a somewhat frantic pace. After all, with the tourist count climbing and those millions of tourist dollars waiting to be spent, a "build them and they will come" attitude prevails.

As a result, there are miniature golf courses, go-cart concessions, and family fun centers galore. Although we'll mention some of these, we'll concentrate on those attractions, activities, and events that are identified with Branson and aren't duplicated in every resort region in North America. Additional attractions are described in chapter 9, Family Values.

Butterfly Place (2400 Highway 165; 417/332-2231). Though you'll see butterflies around Branson's flower beds in summertime, you can watch two thousand of them—representing more than four dozen species—flutter about any time of the year at the Butterfly Place. Each of the colorful plants and shrubs in the greenhouse was selected specifically as a source of nectar. Even if you can't identify any of the plants and don't know a red admiral from a hackberry emperor, being in the midst of this natural beauty is sure to uplift your spirit.

In addition to an exhibit area, there's also an emergence room containing chrysalids of hatching butterflies. Open daily 10 A.M. to 5 P.M., March 24 through October 31; 10 A.M. to 4 P.M., November 1 through December 12. Admission is $7.95 for adults; $5.95 for children ages four through seventeen. A family pass for two adults and two children costs $19.95. Coupons worth $1 off adult admissions ($.50 off children's) can be found in several publications.

Serious photographers are invited to visit from 7:30 to 9:30 A.M., as tripods are not allowed during normal business hours. You definitely won't need a sweater when you're in the greenhouse, where the temperature is kept at eighty degrees, but the rest of the facility is air-conditioned.

Bonniebrook Park (485 Rosie O'Neill Drive; 417/561-2250). This attraction, about nine miles north of town on U.S. Highway 65, is located on the site of the home of Rosie O'Neill, a remarkable woman whose cartoons appeared in such magazines as *Harper's Bazaar* and *Good Housekeeping* during the early twentieth century. O'Neill, who also wrote novels and poems, is best known, however, as the creator of the Kewpie dolls that have been collectors' items for nearly a century (the annual "Kewpiesta" is held in Branson each April).

O'Neill's original home was destroyed by fire in 1947, three years after her death, but it has been re-created by the Bonniebrook Historical Society, Inc., with donations from all over the world. Filled with O'Neill memorabilia, Bonniebrook is listed on the National Register of Historic Places.

Strolling along the park's nature paths is delightful on spring, summer, and fall mornings, and the gardens are a popular setting for weddings and private parties. There are a restaurant and gift shop on the premises, too. Open daily from the first week in March to January, 8 A.M. to 5 P.M.; admission for adults is $5. Children under twelve are admitted without charge. Four tours are conducted hourly in both the morning and afternoon, beginning at 8:30 A.M. and 1 P.M.

At Point Lookout above Lake Taneycomo, **College of the Ozarks** (two miles south of Branson on Highway 65; 800/222-0525 or 417/334-6411) was founded on the premise that students would work at the school to pay their tuition. In the process, the college has not only educated thousands of young people but also developed into one of the area's most interesting tourist attractions.

No full-time students at this unusual college pay tuition; they are involved, rather, in work-study programs. They work in the greenhouses and on construction projects; wait on customers in the gift shop or restaurant. Streets that intersect the pleasant college grounds have been given names like Opportunity Avenue and Industrial Place.

To take a self-guided campus tour, just follow the "Bobcat Trail," a dark red line painted on the walkways that leads you to points of interest. You'll pass the student-staffed Friendship House restaurant, a gift shop where handmade crafts made by students are sold, and Edwards Gristmill, with millstones set against its weathered wood walls. At the mill, powered by a twelve-foot waterwheel, students grind whole grains into flour. On the mill's second floor, other students make rugs, place mats, and other articles on old-fashioned weaving machines.

Working in the fruitcake and jelly kitchen, students produce more than forty thousand cakes a year, along with thousands of jars of jelly and apple butter, which are sold at the school and by mail order. Orchids and houseplants are for sale at the college greehouses, which contain some seven thousand plants. You can purchase the woven items on campus, too.

Ralph Foster Museum, housed in what formerly was a boys' dormitory on the College of the Ozarks campus, is the repository for the collections of radio pioneer Ralph D. Foster. The building's three floors contain everything from mounted birds and butterflies to the Clampett family's jalopy from the *Beverly Hillbillies* TV series of the 1960s. One floor is completely devoted to Foster's fifteen hundred guns—including Pancho Villa's pistols and a Thompson submachine gun. Hunting trophies, in the form of all sorts of mounted animals, line the walls. Rocks and minerals, coins, Native American art and paintings by artists such as Thomas Hart Benton are also on display. The museum is open Monday through Saturday, 9 A.M. to 4:30 P.M. Admission is $4.50 for adults, $3.50 for seniors, and free for people under the age of eighteen.

Ozark Discovery IMAX Theater (3562 Shepherd of the Hills Expressway; 800/419-4832 or 417/335-4832). In this theater with a six-story-high screen—that's ten times the size of the screens in regular theaters—and a twenty-two-thousand-watt sound system with forty-four speakers, viewers are immersed in sights and sounds around them. Productions on subjects from Mount Everest to the Grand Canyon, beavers to whales are featured on the big screen. The theater's signature film, *Ozarks: Legacy and Legend,* is a six-generation saga of the McFarlain family beginning in 1824. Films are shown daily, every hour on the hour from 9 A.M. Admission for adults is $8; for seniors sixty years and over, $7.50; and for children ages four through twelve, $4.95.

The theater is housed in the **IMAX Entertainment Complex,** which also contains a restaurant with adjoining ice cream parlor and bakery and an indoor shopping mall (a bustling area of stalls with tourist-trade items for sale).

A live comedy, the Remember When Show, is presented at the theater complex Tuesday through Saturday. The stage is designed to look like Grandma's attic, filled with old-fashioned furniture, toys, clothes, signs, and bric-a-brac. The theater's lobby is reminiscent of a small-town main street in the 1940s. The show itself is pure nostalgia with large dollops of patriotism and stars Mike Radford, former Kansas City Royals shortstop.

Branson's latest major attraction, the **Veterans Memorial Museum,** is prominently located near the east end of Missouri Highway 76 (1250 West Highway 76; 417/336-2300) and easily identified by the World War II P-51 Mustang fighter plane in front of the building. The eighteen-thousand-square-foot museum, which honors all branches of the military, focuses on the U.S. wars of the twentieth century. Exhibits include Desert Storm camouflage clothing and a rifle used in the Korean conflict. Among the vehicles on display are a World War II motorcycle, a Ho Chi Minh Trail bicycle, and a Cushman motor scooter parachuted on D-Day.

The museum also houses the world's largest war memorial bronze sculpture. It's more than seventy feet long, weighs fifteen tons, and depicts fifty life-sized soldiers storming a beach.

Veterans from each of the fifty states served as models for the sculpture, which was created by the man who owns the museum, Fred Hoppe (Hoppe's father was a soldier in the Second World War). Admission is $11 for adults, $4.50 for children ages six through twelve. Veterans are entitled to a $2 discount.

Although no wine is actually produced at the family-owned and -operated **Stone Hills Winery** (601 Highway 165 and Green Mountain Drive; 417/334-1897), winery tours are offered, during which participants learn about everything from the history of winemaking to an explanation of how bubbles are put into spumante. A wine tasting (juice for the youngsters) follows the tour. There's also a gift shop where you can buy those wines you favor as well as wine-compatible items such as meats and cheeses. The winery is open Monday through Saturday, 8:30 A.M. to dusk; Sunday, 11 A.M. to 6 P.M. The tours, which begin about every fifteen minutes, are free.

At the **Shepherd of the Hills Fish Hatchery** (483 Hatchery Road; 417/334-4865) approximately 1.2 million trout are raised, with 80 percent of them released into Lake Taneycomo. Visitors view trout and other fish eye-to-eye in the aquariums. They can also watch a ten-minute introductory video that explains the spawning process, then take a guided tour of the hatchery at 10 A.M., 11 A.M., 1 P.M. or 2 P.M. weekdays from Memorial Day through Labor Day. On the grounds, a boat ramp and several fishing access points along Lake Taneycomo (where trout fishing is allowed year-round) offer additional recreational options, as do four nature-viewing trails for hikers. The grounds open at 9 A.M., closing at 6 P.M. in summer and 5 P.M. from September through June.

Waltzing Waters (Waltzing Waters Theatre; 3617 Highway 76; 800/276-7284 or 417/334-4144). Promotional materials claim that the computer-driven fountains "choreograph almost 42,000 combinations of water, light, and color to the world's most magnificent musical scores. Teenagers cheer and toddlers are spellbound. Skeptics say, 'It Can't be Water.' Lovers relax and dream. Some folks sing along, and grown men have been known to cry, but no one ever forgets a visit to Waltzing Waters Theatre." The hourly Tuesday through Sunday show is accompanied by recorded music except at 10 A.M.,

1 P.M., and 6 P.M., when an entertainer named Frederick joins the recorded music by playing on two pianos at once. The productions with recorded music cost $6 for adults, $3 for children ages three through eleven. When Frederick's on stage, prices jump to $12 and $6. Although coupons for $1 off the recorded music shows and $2 off the live music performances are in widely distributed brochures, we consider this expensive in comparison with other area attractions.

SPECIAL OCCASIONS

Most of Branson's major celebrations and commemorations center on American culture and history. The best of them take place at Silver Dollar City, a venue for events that are of interest to tourists and residents alike. The monthlong **World-Fest** in April and May is billed as "America's largest international festival." Featuring performers who present the music, dance, and culture of their native lands, the event also offers opportunities to sample ethnic foods and buy crafts from other countries.

The **Great American Music Festival,** held mid-May through the first days in June, presents performances by various musical groups from around the country. The **National Children's Festival** offers dozens of hands-on activities for youngsters at various locations throughout the theme park for two months during summer.

From early September until the last days of October, the **Festival of America** showcases seventy-five or so artisans from around the United States who demonstrate crafts ranging from Amish country woodworking and Shaker box making to Dakota prarie art and California pine-needle basketry.

Another popular setting for special events is downtown Branson. In April, it's the site of an amateur basketball tournament on the street; in May, the **Plumb Nellie Days Hillbilly Festival, Craft Show and Sidewalk Sale.** There's the **50s–60s Street Dance** in June, the **Oldtime Fiddle Contest** in August, and the **Autumn Daze Craft Festival** in September—all of them annual events.

The holiday season brings the **Adoration Parade & Light-**

ing Ceremony (see chapter 9, Family Values) and **Candlelight Christmas,** with carolers and Father Christmas strolling the streets, window decoration contests, and free tree ornament and cookie-making workshops for the children.

A significant number of Branson's special events focus on veterans of the armed services—more than two million of the area's annual visitors have been identified as veterans. There's an **Armed Forces Day** celebration in mid-May, **National Day of Remembrance** service, **Branson Remembers** commemoration each Memorial Day weekend, and **Flag Day** ceremonies on June 14.

In 2001, both the fiftieth anniversary of the beginning of the Korean War (June 25) and Korean War Armistice Day (July 27) were observed, as was POW-MIA Day September 14–16. December events included a Pearl Harbor Worship Service on December 2 and Pearl Harbor Commemoration on December 7.

Among the more unusual special events are the **Mid-America Eagle Watch,** when bald eagles congregate in the Branson area from January through March each year, and **Cruisin' Branson Lights,** when more than two thousand hot rods, classic, customized, and restored vehicles cruise down the strip on an August midnight. There are clogging championships and square-dance festivals, an annual film fest at the IMAX Theater, and a bluegrass festival at Shepherd of the Hills.

Throughout the year, dozens of events like gospel celebrations, motorcycle rallies, local talent shows, food and wine tastings, clogging championships, art shows, and potluck suppers augment the Branson area's year-round attractions.

During November and December, fifteen miles of lights and displays decorate Branson for its annual **Ozark Mountain Christmas.** The **Festival of Lights Parkway** (just off U.S. Highway 65) features a thousand displays and more than seventy-five thousand lights on five hundred Christmas trees. Parades with floats and marching bands follow Missouri Highway 76. Theme parks dress up with greenery and lights—Silver City dazzles with two million lights and a five-story tree. Several of the area's entertainers also offer special holiday shows (see chapter 9, Family Values).

7

Activities

Long before it became a show town, Branson attracted the sort of people who enjoy the active life, for few areas are more conducive to communing with nature or pursuing outdoor sports. Hikers can follow trails through groves of winged elm, post oak, and pignut hickory, along streams and down hillsides bright with columbine, primrose, and wild blue indigo. Fishermen can use every lure in their tackle boxes as they troll the area's lakes. From January through March, it's eagle-watching season, and in summer every water sport from board sailing and scuba diving to Jet Skiing and parasailing is near at hand.

ON THE WATERFRONT

Many of these pleasures result from the region's combination of hills and water. Unlike the rather compact lakes formed by glacial action in the north-central part of the United States, the bodies of water around Branson came into being when dams were built on the White River. As a result, they're mostly irregularly shaped, with lots of squiggles, resulting in an enormous amount of shoreline.

Before 1913, the White River flowed unimpeded through Branson and beyond. Then the Powersite Dam was built east of Branson, forming Lake Taneycomo. Like the river before it, the new lake was a fisherman's warm-water favorite for bass and panfish. But when Table Rock Dam to the west of Branson was completed in 1958, creating another larger, deeper lake, the waters flowed into Lake Taneycomo from the bottom of the new lake, lowering Taneycomo's temperature significantly. Since warm-water fish cannot survive in such cold water, Taneycomo is now stocked with trout, which grow really big (the record for German brown trout caught in Taneycomo was one twenty-three and a half inches long that weighed twenty-five pounds—the largest ever caught using two-pound-test line).

To the northeast, downriver from Branson (the river flows more or less from west to east), the water temperature of Bull Shoals Lake, east of Powersite Dam, is ideal for black, white, striped, largemouth, and smallmouth bass, along with walleyes, crappies, catfish, and bluegills. Several fishing tournaments are held at Bull Shoals throughout the year. These three lakes—Taneycomo, Table Rock, and Bull Shoals, each different from the other—offer a variety of aquatic attractions in addition to fishing.

Lake Taneycomo

Although technically a lake, Taneycomo looks and acts more like a river. It meanders from Table Rock Dam in southwest Branson to the northeast corner of the city limits, providing waterside residential lots, parks, and open spaces; picturesque settings for condominiums and golf courses; and a three-mile stretch of shoreline downtown that is occupied by the city trailer park, waterfront restaurants, small motels, and a handful of commercial boat docks and marinas.

Though the waterfront is far from picturesque, horse-drawn carriages take passengers for rides along the lake during summer. Rides range in length from one-half to three miles and cost from $4 to $10 for adults; $3 to $6 for children. Carriage riding is great for people with tired feet, but those with bad backs may be happier walking.

Most of the area's action goes on a few blocks away in what's called downtown Branson, where more than one hundred independently owned shops, restaurants, and other businesses cater to the daily influx of tourists. More than twenty of the downtown buildings are included on a self-guided map tour (maps are available at the Downtown Branson Mainstreet Association at 120 South Business Highway 65).

Waterfront activity in downtown Branson focuses on sport fishing. All people fifteen years and older who fish in Missouri waters must have a fishing permit. Since both Table Rock and Bull Shoals Lakes straddle the Missouri-Arkansas border, you'll need to be sure you are on the Missouri side of the line if you don't have an Arkansas fishing license.

Daily Missouri permits cost $5; annual permits, $35 for nonresidents (residents, $11). If you fish for trout, you must also have a $7 trout permit. Rainbow and brown trout are the predominant species in Lake Taneycomo, so fishing there requires both a fishing and trout permit, even though you may occasionally catch other species of fish. The best time for catching rainbows is during winter, and top season for browns is fall (locals advise using drifting salmon eggs and angleworms, but only artificial lures are allowed in the area that extends about three miles downstream from Table Rock Dam).

You must also have a fishing permit if you plan to collect frogs, mussels, clams, crawfish, turtles, or live bait. Annual permits, unless noted on the permit itself, are—if purchased on March 1 or after—valid from the date of purchase until the last day of February of the following year. Fishing permits are available at fishing docks and marinas, Wal-Mart, various liquor and convenience stores, and some resorts.

The boat rental companies on Lake Taneycomo are easy to find. They include places like **Scotty's Lake Front Trout Dock,** where you can rent pontoons (a twenty-two-foot pontoon rents for $115 a day; a twenty-eight-footer that seats up to ten people costs $135) and fishing boats ($39 to $45 for a full day; $27.50 to $34 for a half day). If you're looking for a guide, you can find one there, too.

Cruises

The **Lake Queen** (417/334-3015), a genuine paddle wheeler that has cruised Lake Taneycomo for thirty years, departs

How Does Your Catch Measure Up?

According to the *Missouri Fishing Regulations* booklet, the Department of Conservation maintains a list of Missouri state-record fish and recognizes anglers who catch them. To be eligible for an award, your fish must be taken legally and you must:

- Weigh it in the presence of Conservation Department personnel on an accurate scale subject to verification.

- Have your fish identification verified by a Conservation Department agent or fisheries biologist.

    Record fish forms and information are available from the Missouri Department of Conservation.

from the dock at Main Street and North Lake Drive in downtown Branson. There's usually music on the top deck, and the cruises are narrated. Breakfast and dinner cruises as well as three regular cruises operate from the first week in April to the end of October, and there are special Christmas cruises, Friday through Monday, from early November through mid-December. Cruises cost adults $9.84 and children ages three through twelve $6.29. Reservations are required. Also moored on Lake Taneycomo is the *Sammy Lane* **Pirate Cruise** (see chapter 9, Family Values).

Table Rock Lake

Of the three lakes, Table Rock, which has an amazing 857 miles of pristine shoreline and backdrop of wooded hills, is the most developed recreationally, with a number of boat docks and marinas. Its waters, unlike those of Lake Taneycomo, are warm enough for swimming and water sports without wet suits during several months of the year. In most places, however, the lake is surrounded by high limestone bluffs, much like the walls of river gorges. As a result, there aren't many beaches on the lake. Beaches are generally gravel rather than sand.

Table Rock Lake got its name from a rock shelf high above

the White River about a mile downstream from the dam. The U.S. Army Corps of Engineers originally planned to build the dam at that site, but tests showed the place where the giant barrier was ultimately built to be geologically more suitable.

Most of the public marinas at Table Rock Lake are associated with resorts, but are generally open to the public as well. They offer a full complement of water sports, including sailing, Jet Skiing, scuba diving, parasailing, and waterskiing. The condo resorts on the lake have marinas, too, but they're usually for guests only.

Table Rock Lake is recognized as one of the country's top bass fishing lakes, with largemouth, smallmouth, Kentucky spotted, white, and black bass to be caught. You'll catch catfish, too. Spring and late fall are considered the best times to catch bass in shallow water with lures. You can catch crappie in early and midspring and bluegills from late spring to late fall.

One of the most populated areas on Table Rock is Indian Point, a peninsula that juts from the north shore into the lake, where you'll find the largest concentration of lakeside lodging in the form of cabins, cottages, and condominiums. The point is also the location of many of the lake's water sport operations. The road to Indian Point is a continuation to the one that goes to Silver Dollar City, and its farthest location is no more than twenty minutes from Branson.

The other center for water sports and cruises on Table Rock Lake that's close to Branson—only ten minutes from downtown, in fact—is in the Table Rock State Park area. That's where you'll find **Table Rock Dam and Visitors Center** (four miles west of Branson on Highway 76 West and five miles south on Highway 165; 417/334-4104). The marina is one of the best places to rent boats, WaveRunners, and scuba gear. Prices are reasonable, and a $5 discount coupon on rentals there can be found in some of the entertainment guides.

Views of the dam, a nature trail, wildlife exhibits, and audiovisual presentations are features of the center, where visitors can also view bald eagles during the winter months. It's open daily, April through October, 9 A.M. to 5 P.M. Free. Weekday **Table Rock Dam tours** are also available from May through October.

In and on the Water

Visitors can spend time in and the water, even if they're not staying at Table Rock Lake. The most easily accessible public beaches on Table Rock are at **Long Creek, Indian Point,** and **Old Highway 83.** Marinas on the lake that are in the Branson orbit include **Branson Houseboat Rentals** (915 Longcreek Road, Ridgedale; 800/255-5561), **Branson Highway K Marine** (249 Marina Drive, Kirbyville; 417/334-2880), **Lilley's Landing Resort & Marina** (367 River Lane, Branson; 417/334-6380), **State Park Marina** (380 State Park Marine Road, Branson; 417/334-2628), and **Table Rock Marina** (296 Table Rock Marina Road, Branson; 417/338-4433).

Going out on the water, however, can become a fairly expensive proposition unless you have brought your own boat by trailer and can use one of the public access ramps on the lake. The least expensive way, per hour, to get out on the water if you don't have your own watercraft is by renting a fishing boat. You can rent sixteen-foot aluminum boats with fifteen-horsepower motors for about $30 a full day, or bass boats for about $120 at places like **Indian Point Resorts** (51 Dogwood Park Trail; 800/888-1891). But sitting in a boat all day—even if you stop at public beaches now and then—can be rather confining.

Instead, though it isn't cheap, you might want to rent a pontoon. Since daily rental periods include a boat slip at the dock and rental periods usually begin at noon one day and end at 10 A.M. the next, you can come and go as you please throughout the rental period, which in summer gives you about eighteen hours of daylight. The pontoons accommodate twelve people. Daily rental fee at **Table Rock Lake Pontoon Rentals** is $190, with a $20 discount coupon on the company's Web site (www.pontoonrentals.nu). There's also a $100 refundable deposit required. At some marinas, you can rent pontoons at $35 an hour with a two-hour minimum; others have half-day rates from about $90 to $120.

It's also possible to buy packages that combine fishing with accommodations on Table Rock Lake. For example, **Table Rock Lake Resort** (915 Long Creek Road, Ridgedale; 417/334-1413) offers the Fisherman's Dream, which includes two nights' lodging for two people and two days' fishing in a new, fully equipped Tracker bass boat for $335. The Family Getaway package includes three nights' lodging for four, plus one day on a new Tracker pontoon boat for $375.

The simplest solution to spending some time on the water—and sometimes the least expensive—is to patronize the boats docked in the Table Rock State Park area that take passengers out on regularly scheduled cruises.

Best known of the Branson area passenger boats, the paddle wheeler *Showboat Branson Belle* cruises Table Rock Lake with entertainment like that of showboats in the nineteenth century. The dinner cruise show, Steppin' Out, features variety acts including a Russian dance team, a ventriloquist, and the Showboat Quartet. The Rise-n-Shine Breakfast, Family Fun Lunch, Early Escape Dinner, and Sunset Dinner Cruises include entertainment, too, along with three-course meals. The first cruise of the day between April and October includes lunch (11 A.M.; adults, $35; children ages four through eleven, $16). There are also an early dinner cruise at 4:30 P.M. and a Sunset Dinner Cruise at 8 P.M. ($40/$18) During the busy seasons, an 8 A.M. breakfast cruise ($30/$13) is added. (For more information, see chapter 8, Showtime.) The boat leaves from White River Landing, half a mile south of Table Rock Dam on Missouri Highway 165 (800/775-BOAT). On any of the Branson area cruises, when it's possible to take a cruise with or without a meal, opt for the latter. It's more economical and usually more satisfying to eat before or after your boat ride. The main reason, however is that when the excursion includes a meal and entertainment, there's precious little time left to enjoy the views from the deck.

Polynesian Princess (1358 Long Creek Road; 417/337-8366) offers four cruises daily except Monday, April through October. A hula dancer and guitarist provide Polynesian entertainment during the two dinner cruises (departing 5 and 8 P.M., $27). There's also an 11 A.M. sight-seeing-only cruise ($17).

Reservations are recommended, especially in peak season. It's also important to phone in advance at any time because the boat is sometimes chartered for weddings and private functions.

The *Spirit of America* (380 State Park Marina Road; 800/867-2459 or 417/338-2145) docks at the Table Rock State Park Marina. It's a forty-nine-passenger, forty-eight-foot catamaran that takes sightseers on ninety-minute cruises from April through mid-October. Tours depart every day but Monday at noon, 2 P.M., 4 P.M., and dusk. Tickets cost $17 for adults, $7 for children ages five through twelve. Be sure to wear rubber-soled shoes.

Bull Shoals Lake

Though Bull Shoals is the most undeveloped of the three lakes, it offers a variety of water sports activities and public access points. It's a popular fishing tournament lake and has a reputation for producing trophy-sized fish. Record catches include a five-pound, five-ounce white bass; a thirteen-pound, fourteen-ounce largemouth bass; and a twenty-one-pound, one-ounce walleye. It's about a twenty-minute ride to Bull Shoals Lake, which begins at Forsyth, about ten miles from Branson (see chapter 11, Day Trips).

FORE!

If golf is one of your vacation pleasures, you're in luck. Half a dozen area courses, plus several more a bit farther afield, will guarantee great rounds whatever your score. The five courses closest to Branson are:

Branson Creek Golf Club on U.S. Highway 65 South is four miles from town and was designed by Tom Fazio. Eighteen holes of golf cost $55, March 1 through March 31; $85, April 1 through October 31; and $60, November 1 through December 31. Fees include cart, yardage book, bag tag, and range balls. Phone 417/339-4653 or 888/772-9990 to reserve tee times.

Pointe Royale Golf Course is one of three area courses

with lodging facilities on the property. Located on the shores of Lake Taneycomo, it's on Missouri Highway 165 three miles south of Missouri Highway 76. With bent grass greens, Bermuda grass fairways, and challenging water hazards, it's one of the area's most scenic courses. Green fees for eighteen holes on this par-seventy course are $71 (417/334-4477). Guests at RCI time-share properties get discounts.

Thousand Hills Golf Resort is the only golf course within the Branson City limits (245 South Wildwood Drive; 800/864-4145 or 417/336-5873). Rated three and a half stars by *Golf Digest*, the eighteen-hole, par-sixty-four course has a cool-off station that's much appreciated on warm days. Thousand Hills offers nightly condo rentals; there's also a snack bar and restaurant on the premises. Resort guests pay $42 for eighteen holes, while nonguests are charged $62.

Holiday Hills Golf Club (620 East Rockford Drive; 417/334-4443) is the place to go if you're looking for Branson entertainers at play. The par-sixty-eight, eighteen-hole championship course recently underwent a multimillion-dollar expansion and is looking good. The Holiday Hills complex includes a pro shop, full-service resort with nightly condominium rentals, and meeting space. Green fees are $65 before 11 A.M. and $55 after.

Top of the Rock Golf Course (612 Devil's Pool Road; 417/339-5312) is seven miles south of Branson. Boasting "the grandest view in the Ozarks," this is a first of its kind Jack Nicklaus Signature par-three, nine-hole executive course. The course is affiliated with the Audubon Signature Cooperative Program, and 38 percent of its forty-seven acres has been kept in a natural state planted with native trees, grasses, and wildflowers. Green fees are $25 for nine holes ($40 if you go around twice); cart rental costs $7 per nine holes. Rental clubs are available at all the above clubs.

About a forty-five-minute drive from Branson, eighteen-hole, par-seventy **Kings River Golf Course** (Lake Road 37-72, Shell Knob; two miles north of the junction of Highways 86 and 39; 417/858-6330) features tree-lined fairways and undulating grass greens. With coupons found in the Branson newspaper as well as other publications, green fees for two players, including cart and taxes, cost $52.50.

Other area courses include eighteen-hole, par-seventy-one **Stonebridge at Ledgestone** in Branson West (417/336-1786); nine-hole **Oakmont Community Golf Course** (417/334-1572; par thirty-five) in Ridgedale; nine-hole **Taneycomo Golf Club** (417/546-5454; par thirty-five) in Forsyth; and nine-hole **Kimberling Golf Course & Country Club** in Kimberling City (417/739-4370; par thirty-four).

FALL FOLIAGE AND SPRING BLOSSOMS

When autumn comes to the Ozarks, leaf-peepers delight in the reds, golds, and amber added to the landscape. Since there are so many varieties of trees, the array of colors is especially spectacular in the Branson area. One of the most popular fall foliage drives begins thirteen miles east of Branson near Forsyth and goes through the Mark Twain National Forest, the little town of Bradleyville, and the U.S. Forest Service Hercules Glade Wilderness Area, which is also a great hiking spot. In spring, the route is also a splendid one for viewing the dogwood trees in bloom. Maps for the self-guided drive are available at the Forsyth Chamber of Commerce (16075 U.S. Highway 160; 417/546-2741).

EAGLE-WATCHING

Every winter, American bald eagles congregate in the Branson area, nesting in trees, on power-line towers, and in other locations on the bluffs overlooking Table Rock Lake, Lake Taneycomo, and Bull Shoals Lake. During February, two-hour-long guided tours take participants to places where they are likely to see the bird that is our national symbol. The tours are conducted each day from February 1 through February 28, 9 A.M. to 4 P.M. Phone 417/538-2744 for further information.

BICYCLING

Although the Branson area has traffic problems and is hilly—to say the least—there are paths that are less traveled and aren't that hard to negotiate. You will see SHARE THE ROAD signs marking bike paths in town, which makes the busier streets less difficult. One of the most popular rides within the city limits follows Green Mountain Drive from Missouri Highway 165 to Missouri Highway 376. Another Branson ride is a mile-and-a-half mile route that goes between North Beach Park and Sunset Park along the downtown stretch of Lake Taneycomo.

The state park campgrounds offer three miles of paved roads that follow Table Rock Lake's shoreline and loop around the marina. Farther afield at Mark Twain National Forest, hundreds of miles of paved roads as well as four-wheel-drive paths provide lots of riding space. Branson bike shops have maps, books, and other information about the area's best places to ride. They also rent bicycles by the hour, day, and week.

TAKE A HIKE

While hikers are sometimes rewarded with more spectacular views in other parts of the country, no trails can offer more contentment on a fine day than those of the southern Ozarks. Redbud, dogwood, western hawthorn, and wild plum blossom in the spring. Cedar waxwings, mockingbirds, yellow-bellied sapsuckers, and about two dozen other species of birds peck at the red-orange fruit of the hackberry tree, while quail, turkeys, and grouse nibble at the poison ivy. After the first frost, the pale orange fruit of the persimmon trees becomes sweet, and the leaves begin turning color. There's hiking in winter, too, when eagles soar high overhead.

At **Henning State Forest** just west of Branson on Missouri Highway 76 in the White River Hills region (the turnoff is marked RUTH AND PAUL HENNING CONSERVATION AREA), several different trails run through the oak- and hickory-covered hills, ranging in length from one to three miles. There's a small section of bottomland forest along Roark Creek that's delightful for springtime walks. The trees along the trails in the forest are labeled so hikers can get a nature lesson along with their exercise.

Within the Branson city limits, the recently opened **Lake-**

side Forest Wilderness Area (on Fall Creek Road, just south of Highway 76) offers fine views and challenging hiking trails. Trails include one that follows the Lake Taneycomo shoreline. The 130-acre park is also a great place to picnic.

The **Busiek State Forest and Conservation Area,** fourteen miles north of Branson, covers 2,505 acres of steep, rocky hills, and gravel-bottomed creeks. Self-guided nature trails make it easy to commune with the natural world.

The **Drury-Mincy Conservation Area** covers 5,699 acres in southern Taney County (the entrance is off Highway J). The wildlife preserve, with its steep, rocky hills and gravel-bottomed creeks, is a great place for camping and stream fishing as well as hiking, bird-watching, and walking along the self-guiding nature trail. There's also a target shooting area.

Herds of elk, bison, and Texas longhorns roam **Dogwood Canyon,** a ten-thousand-acre privately owned wilderness less than an hour south of Branson. (Take Highway 76 west to the

---

Hiking Reminder

Just because hiking in the area around Branson seems less hazardous than in mountains where the terrain is more rugged, don't forget the safety rules that hikers everywhere should follow:

- Tell a park ranger or other responsible person where you are going and when you expect to be back.

- Stay on marked trails to avoid getting lost.

- Know your limitations. Don't overestimate your physical condition or underestimate your surroundings.

- Wear clothing and shoes or boots appropriate for the weather and the trail.

- Bring along basic first-aid necessities, including insect repellent in summer.

- Learn how to identify any poisonous plants or venomous snakes you might encounter.

- Take extra water and snacks with you, even on short hikes.

junction with Highway 13. Go south to Highway 86 and turn right. The nature park is well marked; 417/335-2777, ext. 7107.) White-tailed deer, wild turkeys, and all sorts of other creatures live at the refuge, too. Rainbow trout are clearly visible, flashing just below the surface of Dogwood Creek. Guided open-air tram tours are available, as are self-guided walking and biking and horseback riding opportunities. There are Civil War and Indian artifact displays; a rustic covered bridge handcrafted by the Amish; and a magnificent waterfall on the premises, too. While it costs $19.95 to take the tram tour and $195 for the guided trout fishing experience, you can walk around the wilderness area for $7.95. It's worth the price, as this is some of the prettiest country in southern Missouri.

8

Showtime

Every day about an hour before showtime, West Missouri Highway 76 becomes a moving parking lot. More often than not, strains of country music waft through the windows of the cars, vans, tour buses, and pickup trucks caught in traffic. One by one, the vehicles peel off to fill the parking lots of the twenty theaters that front on the highway. On Missouri Highways 165 and 248 (Gretna Road and Shepherd of the Hills Expressway), where Branson's other theaters are located, there's action, too, as the theatergoers begin to arrive for the eighty or so performances presented each day.

Though some people describe Branson as "the next thing to Nashville," others claim that the little town at the southern edge of the Missouri Ozarks is the Live Entertainment Capital of the Country or the even more superlative Live Country Music Capital of the World. As they point out, the emphasis in Nashville has changed from performing to recording, so now Branson's the place to go if you want to see live shows—especially those focusing on country music.

Folk music has been performed throughout the Ozarks—on front porches, in churches, and, later, on radio shows—for decades. But it wasn't until 1959, when the four Mabes brothers set up folding chairs in the Branson community hall and put on their Baldknobbers show, that the little town began its evolution into a country music center. Lloyd Presley opened the next theater in 1967, moving his show from its former location at Talking Rocks Cavern, fifteen miles west of Branson.

Success attracted success, and each new season more theaters appeared along the highway. Then, in the late 1980s and early 1990s, country western celebrities like BoxCar Willie, Mickey Gilley, and Mel Tillis built their own theaters. Branson's reputation got a big boost during the latter period when *60 Minutes* on Sunday-night prime time aired a segment on what it dubbed the Country Music Mecca. Since that time, the visitor count—as well as the number of shows—has increased each year.

What qualifies as country music in Branson is everything from mountain music, contemporary country, Cajun, pop, gospel, and bluegrass to cowboy music and jazz. There are combinations, too, like rockabilly—hillbilly music with a rock-and-roll beat. During the 1990s, an influx of performers—mainstream and pop musicians like Andy Williams, Tony Orlando, and Bobby Vinton—tired of traveling and settled down in Branson with theaters of their own. (One caveat to keep in mind, however: Even though a theater bears a well-known performer's name, it's no guarantee that he or she appears in performances there on a regular basis.)

Many of the music halls—especially those established before the 1990s—are small enough that no one is far from the stage, but big enough to hold several hundred people. The largest indoor theaters are Grand Mansion with three thousand seats and Grand Palace with four thousand. While some of the theaters are lavishly decorated, others are high-school-auditorium plain. But whatever the decor, you generally can count on glitz and glitter galore when it comes to the backdrops and costumes.

Each theater's show is different from the others. Although you might think that Branson's early-day shows would be much alike, they're not. Whereas **Baldknobbers Jamboree** (Baldknobbers Theatre, 2835 West Highway 76; 800/998-8908) is pure country western, at **Presley's Country Jubilee** (Presley's Country Jubilee Theater, 2920 West Highway 76; 417/334-4874), entertainment runs the musical gamut from classical piano solos to Dixieland jazz and bluegrass.

Some of the theaters feature two or three entirely different shows a day, while others present as many as five or six different shows during the week. And in most cases, where two or more shows are presented at a theater, they're put on by completely different casts. For example, the Lennon Brothers Swing Music Show entertains in the mornings at the Lawrence Welk Champagne Theatre, while the Welk Show takes the stage for the afternoon and evening performances. Five shows—Jimmie Rodgers Remembers, Legends of Magic, Mike Radford's Remember When Show, Celebrate Sunday with Sue Ann O'Neal, and The Tony Melendez Show—all take place on the stage of the Remember When Theatre in the IMAX Entertainment Complex, while six shows appear on the stage of the 76 Music Hall.

At several of the productions, breakfast or dinner is a part of the package, and tickets include the price of the meal. A few shows offer the option of buying a meal for an additional charge. Ticket prices can vary with the time of day and season, with discount coupons available in a variety of places (see chapter 1, Making Plans).

The season for most theaters runs from April through mid-December, but business became so brisk in the late 1990s that some theaters began to stay open year-round. At any time of year when weather is bad or crowds are thin, however, performances may be canceled.

As you can imagine, parking can be a problem, especially during the busiest times of the year. At performance venues whose parking lots are downhill, such as the Jim Stafford Theatre, shuttles transport showgoers who choose not to make the steep uphill climb. Due to the average age of attendees, parking places for those with disabled placards are all taken well before performance time.

Although their facades and interiors look like theaters, most of Branson's showplaces are actually huge manufactured buildings of corrugated metal. A prime example is the Grand Palace, whose frontal view is that of a gracious southern mansion with imposing white columns and a second-story balcony. The exterior side view, however, reveals what looks like an enormous university fieldhouse tacked on behind the mansion.

The theaters' interior decor ranges from the bare bones—black walls, auditorium-style seats and stage—to elaborate interiors like that of the Grand Palace, Missouri's largest live performance theater and one of its most elaborately decorated. The Grand Palace lobby features a high ceiling with extravagantly embellished chandelier and double staircase. The theater itself, decorated with simple elegance in shades of deep rose and sage green, is equipped with state-of-the-art light and sound systems.

Almost every theater has a gift shop—or at least a small area where CDs, tapes featuring the performers, videos (often including those of the current day's show), and logo items such as T-shirts and caps are for sale. Some of the gift shops are as extensive as those found in the arcades of large hotels, and carry equally wide selections of merchandise. Among the larger operations are the shops at the Shoji Tabuchi Theatre (3260 Shepherd of the Hills Expressway; 417/334-7469) and the Lawrence Welk Champagne Theatre (1984 Highway 165; 800/505-WELK), which covers three thousand square feet. A very small percentage of the items for sale in most of the larger theater gift shops is related to the performers or performances; most of the merchandise is similar to what you would find in any shop that deals in knickknacks, T-shirts, and souvenir items. An exception is the gift shop at the Mel Tillis Theatre, where you can buy Mel Tillis cookbooks and Mel Tillis "Stutterbugs"—hand-painted fishing lures made of basswood in a variety of styles.

Almost every theater also has a food concession in its lobby. These may be as simple as a counter where you can buy soft drinks, coffee, candy bars, and hot dogs or more formal eating areas with tables, chairs, and expanded menus. Several theaters also have restaurants on the premises, which makes it handy for people who want to arrive early in order to get a good parking place.

Not all of Branson's theaters are indoors. At the eight thousand-seat Ozark Mountain Amphitheater, big-name entertainers like Reba McEntire, Waylon Jennings, and Loretta Lynn appear on the season's ten-performance schedule. In another amphitheater a few miles west at Silver Dollar City Crafts Park, a variety of productions have been presented through the years in what has to be one of the Midwest's loveliest settings.

As with the music, there's a good deal of variety in what the performers wear. While many of the men are decked out in traditional cowboy shirts, Texas hats, and bandannas, you'll see everything from tuxedos and white dinner jackets to aloha shirts and beach attire. The women performers often wear dressy country western outfits with lots of sequins and ruffles, but long gowns are popular, too. The opening number of the Jim Stafford show features Stafford in a white suit with a sequined rooster splashed across the front, accompanied by female dancers dressed in extremely unattractive chicken costumes, while he sings a song about the necessity of crowing.

Humor is also an integral part of almost every show. Each cast includes at least one comedian—in many of the shows, it's the traditional country bumpkin with blacked-out teeth who wears mismatched shoes, an oversized tie, and a hillbilly hat. The jokes are corny and often barnyard variety; nonetheless, most people consider these shows suitable for the whole family.

Since there are so many different shows from which to choose, it's a good idea to realize what the range of your options are before you go to Branson. To simplify matters, we have divided the shows into five categories: Celebrity/Star, Family Group, Production/Variety Shows, Musicals, and Miscellaneous.

• **Celebrity/star** performances showcase a single performer. The Grand Palace is Branson's main venue for limited-engagement performances by the big names in country western show business—Lorrie Morgan, Charlie Pride, the Oak Ridge Boys. Among the other celebrities are performers such as Andy Williams, Mel Tillis, and Mickey Gilley, who became big names in decades past, decided to quit traveling, and have built their own theaters in Branson.

The "stars" of some of the shows are performers many of

us haven't heard of before our first Branson visit. One of them is Jennifer (Jennifer's American Theatre; 2905 West Highway 76; 417/335-3664), who energetically sings, taps, and clogs her way through three shows, six days a week. Another is Shoji Tabuchi, who has been in Branson longer than most of the other stars and is undeniably one of the most successful entertainers and entrepreneurs.

• In the **family group** shows, members of one family provide all or almost all of the entertainment. Some of them, such as the Lennon Brothers, have backup bands. The Duttons, the Hughes Brothers, the Brett Family, and the Lowe Family of Utah are among the other families who perform.

Even though they aren't always billed as performers, members of several headliners' families appear on a regular basis in Branson celebrity/star shows. For instance, Mel Tillis's daughters Connie and Carrie April are members of the show's cast, and his grandchildren, although not regulars, frequently perform. Tillis's daughter Pam appears in performances that are announced at the beginning of the season. Both Andy Williams and Glen Campbell, who perform together much of the year (Andy Williams Moon River Theater, 2500 West Highway 76; 800/666-6094), have children who frequently perform in their shows.

• **Production/variety shows** are those in which several groups and individuals—bands, dancers, singers, specialty acts, and soloists—contribute more or less equally to the performance. The shows that started it all, Presley's Country Jubilee and Baldknobbers Jamboree, are perhaps the best-known Branson production/variety shows. More contemporary shows of this type include Cracklin' Rose, Legends in Concert, Country Tonite, the Starlite Kids Review, and 50's at the Hop.

• **Musicals** such as *The Promise, Two From Galilee, Mississippi Love,* and *Nunsense* are rather new to the Branson scene. Although so far, most Branson musicals were first performed somewhere else, *Mississippi Love* was written and produced locally.

• The **miscellaneous** category includes magic shows, ensemble productions like Spirit of the Dance, the Incredible Acrobats of China, the Sunday Gospel Jubilee, and other performances that don't fit precisely into the other categories. For example, while Spirit of the Dance could be considered a production show, it doesn't fall into the typical production/ variety show format.

It isn't possible to go into detail about all the productions currently listed in Branson show guides. We have, however, briefly described a dozen or so of them that have proven popular with a cross section of Branson visitors. Keep in mind that entertainment preferences are subjective: What seems like good value for money to me may not be your idea of what's worthwhile. Remember, too, that theaters are sold, new theaters are built, old shows are scrapped, and new ones take their places. It's a good idea to write ahead to see what's playing when you're going to be in town.

America's funniest immigrant, **Yakov Smirnoff** (Yakov Smirnoff Theatre; 2750 West Highway 76; 800/33-NO-KGB or 417/333-6542) presents top-drawer comedy that appeals to just about everyone. Yakov's humor revolves around his experiences as a new arrival to the United States from Russia. Tales of his confusion with unfamiliar terms and new ways of doing things plus an extremely engaging charisma have proven such a great comedic mix that when other Branson theaters are half empty, Yakov plays to a full house. When Yakov isn't on stage, the Russian dance troupe Neva twirls, leaps, and spins across the stage (Yakov joins them in one number). Authentically costumed, the group complements the production with incredible dancing. Although a second comedian, Slim Chance, is excellent as a juggler—he keeps a bowling ball, Ping-Pong ball, and rubber chicken in the air at the same time—his hayseed role seems to detract from the production. The theater is one of Branson's most appealing, with a Russian theme running through the decor.

The star of the **Shoji Tabuchi Show** (Shoji Tabuchi Theatre; 3260 Shepherd of the Hills Expressway; 417/334-7469), Shoji, has never had a hit record and has made few TV appearances. Nonetheless, he has become a Branson legend and packs in the audiences two times a day from Monday through

Saturday. Charming and charismatic, Shoji puts on a show that well may be the area's number one attraction. One of the most polished productions in Branson, the show achieves a pleasing balance of music, dancing, comedy, and visual effects.

Violinist Shoji's onstage repertoire includes country, Cajun, western swing, bluegrass, and Mozart. Comedian Shoji serves as master of ceremonies when his wife isn't in that role (she's also producer and artistic director of the show). Daughter Christina, who sings and dances, also stars in the production. The Tabuchis are supported by an excellent band and polished dance company whose routines encompass everything from polkas to ballet.

Not only is the show highly recommendable, the Shoji Tabuchi Theatre, styled after the movie palaces of the 1930s, is one of Branson's most interesting (there's even a soda fountain in the lobby). A must-see is the women's rest room, which gives new meaning to the term *overdecoration*. From its Empire-period ceiling and tiled floor to the jewel-glass, extravagant chandeliers and cut orchids at each onyx-and-granite pedestal basin, it may be the most heavily embellished room of its kind in the United States.

As at most Branson shows, any night you'll find a number of locals in the audience. At Shoji's, one of them well might be Rosie, a salesperson at Carolina Mills, who by September 23, 2001, had seen the show twenty-eight times since the first of the year.

Lennon Brothers Swing Music Show (Welk Champagne Theatre; 1984 Highway 165; 800/505-9355 or 417/337-7469) is one of the most refreshing, upbeat shows in Branson. And unlike most period pieces, the brothers—Dan, Bill, and Joe—along with Bill's wife Gail, authentically re-create the 1940s style. From the flower in Gail's hair to her nonmatching rhinestone choker and bracelet, costuming is superb and just right. The choice of tunes reminds members of the audience old enough to remember of Paula Kelley and the Modernaires, the Pied Pipers, and the Delta Rhythm Boys. In one segment of the show, the singers do great imitations of such vocalists as Jo Stafford, Peggy Lee, and Bing Crosby. They're backed up by the well-rehearsed Lennon Brothers Band. The entire show, in fact, is a total package and one of the best entertainment values in Branson. *Tip:* Skip the breakfast, since it's served in another room before the show.

The Duttons (Dutton Family Theatre; 3454 West Highway 76; 888/388-8661 or 417/332-2722) are an attractive and gifted family, and they've worked very hard to perfect their musical skills. The story goes that the parents, a university economics professor named Dean and his wife Sheila, wanted their seven children—all born within nine years—to learn discipline and to work together. In pursuit of these goals, the children started taking violin lessons when they were between the ages of three and five years. As time went by, they learned to sing, dance, and play a variety of instruments. The result is one of the most inspiring and warmhearted shows in town. Though the focus is on bluegrass and country music, the depth of their ability is best displayed when the accomplished group (including Mom and Dad) plays classics like Johann Pachelbel's Canon in D. Among the family's credits are thousands of concerts worldwide and a national PBS television special.

Spirit of the Dance (Bobby Vinton Theatre; 2701 West Highway 76; 888/GO-BRANSON or 417/334-2500), like its counterpart productions that have become so popular in North America, takes Irish step-dancing to a level that transcends the original form. Performed by the Irish International Dance Company, most of the numbers—including, believe it or not, a hoedown—involve ensemble work. Still, principal dancers get a chance to shine in some of the jazz, ballet, flamenco, and salsa-flavored dances. There are vocals, too, along with Irish fiddle playing. The glittery women's costumes depart from the traditional by baring the shoulders, but retain the trademark black tights. Male dancers are clad in the usual T-shirt-type tops, black trousers, and shoes.

Lawrence Welk Show (Welk Champagne Theatre; 1984 Highway 165; 800/505-9355 or 417/337-7469) brings back Saturday-night television of the 1950s and 1960s. Accordion whiz Tim Padilla, with a Lawrence Welk kind of smile on his face during the entire performance, plays the sort of tunes Welk did. The twenty-piece Lawrence Welk Orchestra, conducted by John Bahler, has the same sound as fifty years ago when it plays tunes like "The Beer Barrel Polka." The Russian dance duo of Pasha and Alyona dance through the tango, polka, and jitterbug numbers every bit as gracefully as the featured Welk dancers of long ago. And then there are the Lennon Sisters, more than forty years older than they were when they first appeared on the *Welk Show*. The three sisters who appear in the show—Kathy, Janet, and Mimi—are still in top form, captivating the audiences with a medley of three of their signature songs, "My Man," "Danny Boy," and "How Are Things in Glocca Morra?" Out of six Welk Singers and Dancers, one is Janet Lennon's daughter and another is Peggy Lennon's son. Needless to say, the show has all the polish and professionalism you would expect, and the two thousand three hundred-seat Champagne Theatre provides an excellent venue for it.

Dolly Parton's Dixie Stampede Dinner and Show (Dixie Stampede; 1525 West Highway 76; 800/520-5544 or 417/336-3000) is a show that's among the most popular with the youngsters. Although Dolly isn't part of the show, she reportedly makes an occasional appearance. Thirty-two horses are the show's stars. They appear in buckboard races and drawing carriages containing gentlemen and southern belles; in acts with trick riders and ropers; and in a "friendly" war between the North and South as well as in a star-spangled patriotic finale. There are ostrich and pig races, too. The meal—chicken, barbecued pork, corn on the cob, biscuits, potato, pastry, and beverage—was devised so that cutlery isn't necessary. The audience sits around the arena in tiered rows with counter-type dining ledges. Even if you don't attend the show, you can meet the horses from 10 A.M. until showtime without spending a dime.

Country Tonite (Country Tonite Theater; 4080 West Highway 76; 800/468-6648 or 417/334-2422) played in Las Vegas before it moved to Branson. Some changes have been made—notably that semi-bare bottoms have been covered and costumes generally have become less revealing—but the show has lost none of its high-energy dazzle. Costuming is clever, and the level of musicianship is high. Not only are the piano player and fiddler extremely competent, but a world-class yodeler, great guitar player, and expert rope twirler are also members of the ensemble. The Country Tonite dancers add excitement, especially when they show off the Ozark-style clogging that has become a Country Tonite trademark. It's apparent why the show was voted Best Live Country Music Show in America by the Country Music Organization of America for three years in a row.

Mississippi Love (Mark Twain Theatre; 470 Highway 248; 417/337-8900) made its debut in September 2001 with guest star Debby Boone and a cast of thirty—many of whom are children and teenagers. The story begins where *The Adventures of Tom Sawyer* left off, with Mark Twain beginning to write a sequel, which is censored after each day's work by his wife. Characters include members of the Ladies' League, a couple of incompetent con men, Tom Sawyer, Huck Finn, some extremely talented high-school-aged dancers, and a chorus of children who sing as well together as any we have heard. Stage sets are super, costuming is attractively professional, and the show—despite a rather thin plot and a bit of overacting here and there—one of the best in Branson.

Cracklin' Rose (Remington Theatre; 3701 West Highway 76; 800/595-1301 or 417/336-1220), one of Branson's newest productions, showcases the tunes made famous by Neil Diamond. An energetic cast of singers and dancers plus a seven-piece orchestra work their way through songs like "Kentucky Woman," "I Am I Said," "Song Sung Blue," "Solitary Man," and, of course, "Cracklin' Rose." This full-stage revue gets much of its punch from the enthusiasm of the performers and variety of tunes, from ballads like "You Don't Bring Me Flowers " to the unforgettable "Sweet Caroline." Costuming is cute rather than flashy, and there's a pleasant casualness to the entire production, even though it has been performed in two of Branson's most formal theaters—the Grand Palace and the Remington.

The **Mel Tillis and Family** show (Mel Tillis Theater; 2527 Highway 248; 417/335-M-MEL) celebrated its twelfth Branson season in 2001. For thirty years before settling down, Tillis traveled with his Statesiders band, playing more than two hundred dates a year. His Branson show has proved extremely durable, with Mel, his daughters Connie and Carrie, the State-siders, backup singers, dancers, and occasionally his grand-children appearing in the production.

Tillis opened his two thousand seven hundred-seat the-ater—the large red building resembles a round Dutch barn—in April 1994. The interior, designed in the style of the old Fox Theatres, contains state-of-the-art sound and light systems. A new recording studio is also part of the complex. Showtimes are at 2 and 8 P.M. Tuesday through Sunday. Tickets cost $29 ($15 for children) during the regular season and $32 for the Christmas show.

The Promise (Promise Theatre; 755 Gretna Road; 417/336-4202) is a favorite with the many church groups that travel by bus to Branson. The story of the life of Jesus Christ is given a western spin: The narrator is a cowboy who is at his best when he is singing. The performance itself begins with the nativity, in which a beautiful, immaculately costumed Mary sings "Si-lent Night" to the baby Jesus. Subsequent scenes feature the wise men and shepherds as well as the young Jesus in the tem-ple. Then a fully grown Jesus with blond, blow-dried hair, ap-pears in a scene where he is baptized by his cousin, John the Baptist. In ensuing scenes, the devil, dressed all in red—hat, frock coat, breeches—appears, sitting in a tree, mingling with the crowd, tempting Christ as he performs his miracles. The Passover feast, betrayal by Judas Iscariot, crucifixion, and res-urrection are equally literal in their interpretation. Spectacu-lar costuming, lighting, and set designs; live animals; and flying angels are all part of a production that will appeal most to people who believe in an absolutely literal interpretation of the Bible and are comfortable with a squeaky-clean, non-Semitic Christ.

Starlite Kids Revue (Starlite Theatre; 3115 West Highway 76; 877/336-STAR or 417/337-9333) spotlights astonishingly talented youngsters from ages six to sixteen. They hold their microphones like old pros, belting out their songs with poise that some adult entertainers never achieve. Whether the num-ber involves half a dozen dancers, a six-year-old songstress, or a juvenile comedy team, this show wows people of all ages.

Since the show goes on at 5:30 P.M., it's a great one for younger children to watch.

Two different productions, **Cirque Fantastique** and **Steppin' Out,** are presented on the *Showboat Branson Belle* (4800 Highway 165; 800/775-BOAT). Cirque Fantastique, which is the lunch show, features Russian acrobat Andrei and his wife Marina, who danced with Moscow's Bolshoi Ballet for eight years. Also in the cast is their twelve-year-old son, a whiz on the unicycle, juggler Michael Chirrick, and host/comedian Bob Nichols. The dinner cruises feature the musical Steppin' Out, which salutes America's favorite movies. Similar to cruise ship revues, the show's highlights include adagio dancers Elena and Vadim Serykh and a six-piece stage band. The cast also includes a quartet of singer/dancers, a ventriloquist/comedian, and singer/host (see chapter 7, Activities, for prices).

While not expensive as far as dinner shows in other areas are concerned, in our opinion you will get more value for your money by spending a bit more. Instead of the dinner cruise, take a sight-seeing cruise, see a Branson show, and eat at the restaurant of your choice. That way you can spend your time on the water enjoying the scenery, eat what you wish to order, and see a show with fewer distractions.

One of the most relaxed stars on the Branson stage is **Jim Stafford** (Jim Stafford Theatre; 3440 West Highway 76; 417/335-8080). After the opening number, mentioned above, Stafford sings, plays the guitar and tells stereotypical jokes, often reinforcing the notions that women's most gratifying occupation is telling their husbands what to do and that men repair everything with duct tape. Like many of the performers who are working to instill the tradition of show business in their children, Stafford includes a rather long video of his four-year-old daughter, Gee Gee, as part of one number. Gee Gee also appears on stage, as does her brother, an eight-year-old who plays the drums.

Whatever the show's format or costuming, it's a tradition at intermission (and often before the show begins) for the master of ceremonies to hawk items such as the T-shirts, bandannas, caps, photos, and tape recordings that are for sale at the theaters' souvenir stands and gift shops. At the intermission or end of some of the shows, members of the cast come out to sit on the edge of the stage and chat with members of the audience as they file by. Yakov Smirnoff spends intermissions autographing copies of his books (hundreds of them are purchased each day) and posing for pictures with their purchasers. Despite the hundreds of people the shows' performers shake hands with, talk to, and autograph souvenir items for, they manage to remain as approachable as the folks next door.

Much of the shows' popularity, it would seem, derives from that approachability. Most Branson shows have Web pages on the Internet. While the pages featuring the majority of the shows are traditional, those of the family shows are more in the format of fan club pages. They include extensive information and photos of each of the performers/family members (if they are married, their spouses and children are pictured, too). The Web site of the Lowe Family of Utah, for example, includes separate pages for the mother, father, their son, and each of their six daughters—whose names all begin with the letter *K*. The clan's grandmother has a page, too, and there's a three-page gallery of family pictures taken through the years.

HOLIDAY SHOWS

The holiday season has become what may be Branson's biggest time of the year. In addition to the displays of lights and special events (see chapter 6, Attractions, and chapter 9, Family Values), many of the theaters feature special holiday shows. This is the time when celebrities and stars really pull out the stops in showcasing their families. The Lawrence Welk Christmas Show—like the Lawrence Welk TV shows of the 1950s and 1960—is devoted to presenting the performers' youngsters in musical numbers. And since the Lennon Sisters, as well as other members of the TV show cast, now have children *and* grandchildren, there are a lot of kids to showcase.

Since the holiday shows began, the **Andy Williams Christmas Show** (Andy Williams Moon River Theater; 2500 West Highway 76; 800/666-6094) has been a favorite. It's somewhat of a musical documentary, with Williams and his guests reminiscing and performing Christmas songs, including those Williams recorded on his Christmas album years ago.

Another annual show that's extremely popular is the **Radio City Christmas Spectacular Starring the Rockettes** (Grand Palace; 2700 West Highway 76; 800/884-4536 or 417/336-1220). Whether they're dressed in green and red Santa costumes or ball gowns with six-foot-wide hoop skirts, whether they're tap dancing or going through a high-kicking chorus routine, these precision dancers enthrall their audiences. The show's highlight is the Rockettes' traditional Parade of the Wooden Soldiers, which ends with the dancers falling down like dominos.

BUYING TICKETS

When you or your group travel to Branson independently, you can take several approaches to buying tickets for the shows you want to see. If you want to have your show tickets arranged prior to arrival in Branson, you can order them from any one of dozens of ticket services. There will be a charge—usually about $2 to $2.50 per ticket if you are to pick them up at the theater box office (you'll be sent a voucher by the ticket agency). Ticket delivery to your hotel will cost about $3 per ticket.

A second option is to call the theater box offices where your chosen shows are playing. You will be asked to guarantee your purchases with a credit card. It is then your responsibility to pick up the tickets at least an hour before showtime. Since most show tickets are nonrefundable, you'll be out the purchase price if you have to cancel your plans.

Unless you buy a trip package that includes show tickets and also purchase trip cancellation insurance, the least expensive way of purchasing tickets is to wait until you arrive in town. Check out promotions and any coupons you can find. On most shows you'll save a minimum of $2 on each ticket, and possibly a good deal more. Go personally to the theater ticket offices (not at showtime), look at the seating charts, and buy the tickets from a selection of what's available.

Ticket prices generally range from $17 to $39, with a few shows costing less. Most Christmas shows cost about $2 more than the regular performances. Surprisingly, some of the best shows, such as Shoji Tabuchi (adults, $31 regular, $36 Christmas; children, $20/$22), Yakov Smirnoff ($27.50; children twelve and under, free), the Lennon Brothers Swing Music Show ($19.95; children, free), and the Duttons (adults, $19; family tickets, $39), are not among the most expensive.

Since discount coupons are widely distributed for every show, you can count on saving at least $1 and more often $2 on each ticket. Coupons for new shows such as Cracklin' Rose ($2.50 discount) are usually for larger amounts than those for established productions.

The one problem with this do-it-yourself approach is that the show you most want to see will no doubt be a sellout. There's still hope, however, because most theaters release reserved tickets that haven't been picked up about an hour before curtain time.

Personal Recording Star Time

After you have seen a show or two, you may decide to become a recording star by making a cassette or CD at **Singing Sensations** (Grand Village; 417/335-4435). It's really quite simple. All you do is choose from a list of more than four hundred songs—gospel, country, standards, and pop rock—go into your own private booth, and practice singing along with a recording made by a professional. You can do "I Fall to Pieces" à la Patsy Cline; sing "I Cross My Heart" along with George Strait or croon "Oops . . . I Did it Again" with Britney Spears. After recording your song—still singing with the celebrity—the technicians get to work. They erase the professional's voice, so it's only you on the finished tape or CD. You can record one song on a cassette for $14.95, and as many as ten songs for $86.95. CD recording prices start at $22.95 for one song. You can also make recordings using background music only for $8.95 for the first song; $7 for each additional song on the same tape. Prices include personalized labels.

ENTERTAINMENT PACKAGES

Companies like **Branson Nights** (800/329-9999; www.bran sonnights.com) offer packages that allow clients to choose among about a dozen and a half hotels and motels, pairing their accommodation selection to whatever shows they may want to see. The price of the package is computed by totaling the packager's cost of the accommodations and tickets as well as a commission.

Like several of the shows, Baldknobbers Jamboree offers packages that include accommodations—in this case at the Baldknobbers Motor Inn—and meals (two free dinners at the Baldknobbers Restaurant) in addition to show tickets. In 2001, the package cost $99.99 for two people sharing a room. Since show tickets cost $21.50 each, price for the room and two dinners figures out to $56.99.

9

Family Values

Families who enjoy a combination of natural and man-made attractions can save a bundle in Branson. Not only are accommodations and meals reasonably priced, but the Branson area also offers several vacations' worth of free or low-cost attractions and activities that both adults and children will enjoy. Fortunately for parents' pocketbooks, most of the shows are free or have special prices for children—and youngsters under the age of six get in free. Although there are overabundant go-cart and arcade game attractions, almost all other entertainment is low-cost when compared with that offered at other popular holiday destinations.

GETTING THERE

To get your trip off to a good start when you're flying to Branson, find out in advance what choices the airline offers for children's meals. Most airlines have dishes such as pizza, chicken nuggets, and hamburgers that appeal to young palates, but you have to order them at least twenty-four hours before takeoff time. Getting seat assignments early will help ensure that you get the window seats kids love.

Most airlines give young passengers coloring books and other toys to help keep them busy during flights, but you might have each child pack his or her backpack with a few cherished toys as well. Most older children and teenagers stay happily occupied with headphones, their favorite tapes, and handheld games. And if you're traveling with little ones, remember to pack bottles, "sippy cups," and pacifiers to ease inner ear pressure during takeoffs and landings.

If you're traveling by car and dreading the nonstop skirmishes in the backseat, spend some of your pretrip planning on keeping the children occupied. One solution is to rotate seats every couple of hours, so that the kids take turns riding in the front passenger seat. Another way to sustain a tranquil mood is to supply each child with a package containing new activity books, toys, and other items—all individually wrapped—that they can open every hour or so. If children are old enough, have them come up with ideas for car games they would like to play.

When you're packing, let the kids help you choose the clothes they're going to wear. So what if they don't match? Chances are you won't see anyone you know, and you'll avoid the clothes hassles that can make days start out all wrong. To save the children (or you) time finding what they need, pack each outfit—complete with socks and underwear—in a large plastic zipper-lock bag. Bring along a mini first-aid kit containing Band-Aids, antibiotic ointment, and children's aspirin that will easily fit into an adult's pocket.

ACCOMMODATIONS ADVICE

Whether you decide to stay in Branson or at accommodations on Table Rock Lake will depend largely on your family's interests. Families planning to see several shows and do a lot of shopping or sight-seeing will most likely want to stay close to the in-town attractions. Those interested primarily in outdoor activities, with plans to see only one or two shows, will probably be happier finding a place to stay that's away from the crowds. A number of properties, both in town and on the lake, allow two children to stay in a room with their parents at no extra charge. Rates are so reasonable compared to most other popular vacation spots, however, that you might want to splurge on a separate room for the youngsters.

Finding open spaces where children can run off excess energy won't be a problem even in town. Several of the lodging places have playgrounds on the premises, and there are fourteen parks in the Branson area, many with tennis courts, picnic areas, and paths for jogging.

SELECTING SHOWS

Although all the shows in Branson are marketed as "family-suitable," some of them will be far more popular with the kids than others (see chapter 8, Showtime). Some of the newer theaters have "time-out" areas, a boon to parents with crying babies. The rooms, located at the rear of the theaters, are glass-fronted and soundproof. Sound systems allow parents to hear as well as see the show while their toddlers are throwing their tantrums.

KID-PLEASING ATTRACTIONS

Like any popular vacation spot, Branson has more than its share of attractions that children will look at with longing. Fortunately, discount coupons are available for most of them, which reduces the cost somewhat.

Ripley's Believe It or Not Branson Museum (3326 West Highway 76; 417/337-5460) specializes in the bizarre. This becomes obvious as soon as you see the facade of its building, which looks like it's in the throes of an earthquake. Inside, examples of the biggest, oldest, tallest, and tiniest of everything from garden vegetables to the world's largest ball of nylon string are somewhat reminiscent of the carnival "freak shows" of days gone by.

There are twenty-six Ripley museums around the world, but each of them has a different assortment of exhibits. The Branson displays include items of local interest such as a candy bar that survived the Mickey Gilley Theatre fire of 1993 intact. And don't miss the full-sized limousine with a heart-shaped Jacuzzi built into the trunk. There's the exhibit featuring a sixty-year-old Japanese sailor who spent three months alone while crossing the Pacific in a yacht made out of beer kegs, a handheld computer shaped like a pen, and an inflatable outdoor sofa that squirts water to keep its occupant cool. The themed galleries include country music, primitive, marine, oddities, collections, illusions, and Ripley's study.

Among the displays are a painting of the four Beatles on a grain of rice and a large jelly-bean portrait of Mary Poppins, as well as paintings on potato chips and a huge carving made out of camel bones. Probably the most unusual of the exhibits are a shrunken human head from Ecuador and a fourteen-foot-tall, nine-foot-long "Chinese Dragon Ship" carved entirely of jade—one of only eight in the world. Open daily; hours vary. Admission for adults is $12.95; for children, $7.45. You'll find two different Ripley discount coupons. One is for $2 off adult admissions. The other allows $1.50 off an adult's on $1 off a child's ticket.

The facade of the **Hollywood Wax Museum** (3030 West Highway 76; 800/720-4110 or 417/337-8277) is patterned after Mount Rushmore. Instead of faces of former presidents, however, it's adorned with larger-than-life faces of dead movie stars—Marilyn Monroe, John Wayne, Charlie Chaplin, Elvis Presley.

Inside the museum, you're greeted by a sixty-foot-tall King Kong. The displays that follow run the wax-figure gamut from the Hall of Presidents and Land of Oz to the Grand Ol' Opry and the Last Supper. The Crypt Room (it's really creepy) holds an alien, Elvira, Dracula, and Jason of *Friday the 13th*. In a sunnier scene, baseball great Mark McGwire stands ready to send one out of the park.

There are 170 figures in all, so it takes a while to see them all. It's open daily 8 A.M. to midnight. Tickets cost $9.95 for adults; children ages six through eleven, $6.95; free for children five years and under. Look for $1 and $2 discount coupons in brochures. The $1 coupons are widely distributed, but I was able to find $2 coupons in the *Shepherd of the Hills Gazette*.

Although the majority of Branson's visitors are seniors, it isn't surprising that the **World's Largest Toy Museum** (3609 West Highway 76; 417/332-1499) has arrived in town. Housed in a ten-thousand-square-foot building, the museum contains thousands of playthings that span the generations dating back to the 1880s.

Lionel train layouts, pedal cars, Mickey Mouse and Shirley Temple memorabilia; toy stoves and doll dishes; GI Joes and matchbox toys are all on display, assuring that children, their parents, and their grandparents can find their favorites in the huge collection.

One of the crowd pleasers is a diorama of Dickens' *A Christmas Carol* that was displayed in a Galveston, Texas, department store during the 1930s. Another is the display of lunch boxes—remember the Little Mermaid? The doll exhibits include those with porcelain faces from Victorian times to a host of Barbies. There's a huge collection of cap guns—about five hundred of them—along with a Lone Ranger costume and an array of BB guns.

The museum is open 9 A.M. to 9 P.M., Monday through Saturday. Admission is $8.95 for adults, $6.95 for children. Discount coupons for $2 off adult and $1 off child admissions are part of the museum's ads in many of the free entertainment publications.

When temperatures sizzle, you'll either want to head for air-conditioned theaters, a lake, or twelve-acre **White Water,** the Ozarks' largest water park (3305 West Highway 76; 417/334-7487). Creating white water thrills, Paradise Plunge is a slide with a 207-foot triple drop. You can tube down the Lazy River or body surf in Surfquake, the half-million-gallon wave pool. Splash Island, designed especially for kids, includes a play area for tots called Little Squirts' Waterworks. It's an aquatic wonderland of nozzles, wheels, spouts, and sprays on a nonslip surface. There's also an interactive family attraction called Raintree Island, which features slides, geysers, and a seven-hundred-gallon spinning bucket. Open daily mid-May through August, 9 A.M. to 8 P.M. Daylong passes cost adults $24; ages fifty-five-plus, $12; children ages four through twelve, $19 (prices do not include tax). You can often find discount coupons, and White Water tickets can also be bought as part of Silver Dollar City packages.

Sammy Lane **Pirate Cruise** (280 North Lake Drive; 417/334-3015; www.bransoncruises.com) is another option for cooling off. This seventy-minute narrated cruise on Lake Taneycomo has a certain amount of kid appeal since it includes a stop at a gold mine and a pirate fight. One of Missouri's oldest continuously operating attractions, the *Sammy Lane*—named after a heroine in *Shepherd of the Hills*—has been in business since 1913. Cruises are offered daily from mid-April through October with various departure times. Prices are $10.95 for adults; $7 for children three through twelve years. Reservations are required.

The paddle wheels *Lake Queen*, with breakfast and dinner as well as sight-seeing cruises, and *Polynesian Princess*, which cruises Table Rock Lake, provide other on-the-water attractions (see chapter 7, Activities). There's entertainment on both boats. **Ride the Ducks** and the **Branson Scenic Railway** (see chapter 4, Getting Around) are other modes of transportation that children like a lot.

Gotcha Laser Tag & Arcade (3107 West Highway 76; 417/332-2522) is not inexpensive, but might be worth it when the kids get restless on a rainy day. The action takes place in a black-lighted arena, laid out like a maze. Players, equipped with special laser vests, play as individuals or in teams with the object of "tagging" the opposition with their laser guns. Each player's goal is to make it through the maze without being "tagged out." Open daily from 10 A.M. to midnight (earlier closing in January and February); rates are $7 for one round, but cost less in winter.

The Track, with five Branson locations; **Ridge Runner Family Fun Center** (3450 West Highway 76; 417/335-4085); **Kids Kountry** (2435 West Highway 76; 417/334-1618); **Pirates Cove** (2901 Green Mountain Drive; 417/336-6606); and **Thunder Road** (3235 West Highway 76; 417/334-5905) offer go-carts, mini golf, and game arcades. There's also indoor miniature golf at Grand Country Square (1945 West Highway 76; 417/334-3919) and **Lost Treasure Golf** (3346 West Highway 76; 417/332-0889).

VERY SPECIAL EVENTS

Children's activities are part of the many special events and festivals held throughout the year. The Fourth of July parade

Kiddie Coupon Clippers

You like to save money, but you hate fussing with coupons. Why not have the kids do it? Children who are able to read can be in charge of collecting the discount "two-fers" (two for the price of one) and buy-one-get-one-free coupons that are so plentiful in Branson. The only equipment you'll need to provide are scissors for each of the coupon clippers and envelopes to put the coupons in. If they label the envelopes FOOD, TREATS, ATTRACTIONS, SHOWS, and SHOPPING, it will be easier to find the coupons when you need them.

Since there are brochure racks and free entertainment publications in many locations—motel lobbies, car rental agencies, restaurant foyers, in racks at supermarkets—looking for coupons will give the youngsters something to do while you're waiting in lines. And looking through the entertainment magazines and tabloids provides a good quiet-time activity. Among the coupons they'll find that the whole family can use are for **Ride the Ducks** and the **Branson Scenic Railway** (see chapter 4, Getting Around). Every go-cart, mini golf attraction has discount tickets in several publications.

The Track, which has five locations on Missouri Highway 76, offers a GO-Card, which will work only for large families, residents, or kids with lots of money to spend. After buying forty-eight tickets at $1 each, the GO-Card saves 50 percent on each subsequent ticket purchased for a year. Other of the Track's coupons make more economic sense for the one-time visitor. They include "buy one mini golf, get one free" and "buy two rides, get one free" coupons. **Lost Treasure Golf** offers a $1-off-per-person family coupon that's good for games until 5 P.M. **Pirate's Cove** coupons offer $1 off for each golfer. **Raiders Run** and **Thunder Road** (next to Pirate's Cove) have "two go-cart rides for the price of one coupons."

and community-sponsored events that include activities like street dances and street basketball, though not specifically designed for kids, provide free fun. The largest child-oriented celebration of its kind in the country, the **National Children's Festival,** takes place at Silver Dollar City from June 10 through August 20 each year. Hands-on kids' crafts like sand art, basketry, and tie-dye; pie-eating contests; Lego play areas;

henna painting; scrapbook art; and a backyard circus are among its most popular events.

CHRISTMAS IS FOR KIDS

The magic of millions of lights shimmering in the winter sky, Santa arriving by carriage decorated with pine boughs and red ribbons, an illuminated nativity scene with forty-foot-high figures, and a parade that's been a part of the season for fifty-one years all create a Branson holiday celebration that's special.

When the Branson area **Festival of Lights** begins the first of November and continues through New Year's Day, Missouri Highway 76 is illuminated with more than three hundred stars. A giant polyhedron star shines down from Mount Branson. Static displays sparkle along the Taneycomo lakefront, at Thousand Hills on Green Mountain Drive, and on Indian Point Road. The centerpiece of the light show, however, is the Festival of Lights Parkway, a two-mile drive that features more than seventy-five thousand lights, five hundred Christmas trees, and thousands of static and animated displays.

Nearby, **Silver Dollar City** has its own extravagantly illuminated tree, Christmas lights, and special events. The Trail of Lights drive-through at **Shepherd of the Hills** offers a variety of holiday scenes, and **Branson USA** presents its Holiday Light Spectacular with more than a million lights. They're all part of the Ozark Mountain Christmas celebration, which also includes Springfield, Forsyth, and other towns in the region.

Branson's historic **Adoration Parade** takes place downtown on the first Saturday of December. Preparade activities start at about 3 P.M. with live entertainment including a Christmas carol choir. The parade features dozens of marching bands decked out for the season, floats, and other festive entries. After the parade, the enormous nativity scene atop Mount Branson is illuminated.

Almost every show in Branson has a "spectacular" that's presented during the holiday season, too. Youngsters especially enjoy performances such as the **Lawrence Welk, Mel Tillis,** and **Andy Williams/Glen Campbell** shows, which include special numbers featuring the performers' children and grandchildren.

Children who have saved their holiday shopping money for the trip will find lots of places to buy gifts—from **Dick's Old-time 5 & 10,** the big dime store in downtown Branson, to handcrafted items at **Shepherd of the Hills Homestead** and **Silver Dollar City.**

Information about the areawide Ozark Mountain Christmas and maps indicating the locations of Festival of Lights displays are available at the Branson Chamber of Commerce Visitors Center on Missouri Highway 248.

SHOPPING SPECIALS

Any time of the year, pint-sized shoppers won't want to miss stores like **Storybook Treasures** (Grand Village, 2800 West Highway 76; 417/336-7212), **K-B Toy Liquidators** (Factory Merchants of Branson, 1000 Pat Nash Drive, #B6; 417/335-8047), and the **Doll Depot & Gift Box** (112 Commercial Street; 417/335-4438). At the **Card Shop** (1213 East Main Street; 417/335-4330), collectible cards—baseball, football, basketball, and soccer—are the main attractions. They also carry Disney and fantasy cards.

Make a list of the attractions and shopping opportunities that appear above, and add the attractions, activities, shopping, and shows described in previous chapters that appeal to children. When you get to Branson and the kids ask, "What do we do next?"—you'll have plenty of answers.

10

The Senior Scene

There's no doubt about it. Many of North America's popular destinations—the Disney worlds and lands and downtowns, Six Flags Over Everywhere, the Las Vegas Strip, San Francisco, New York City—cater to young families or hip singles, upwardly mobile baby boomers and those who have already arrived. But Branson is not like those destinations. It's primarily a senior sort of place. Especially for seniors who are looking for ways to stretch their vacation dollars.

Grounded in the tradition of the Grand Ol' Opry and Red Foley's TV show of the 1950s called *Ozark Jubilee,* the majority of Branson's musical shows focus on classic country music. The accent of several other productions such as the Welk Show and the Lennon Brothers is on TV-type entertainment of the 1950s and 1960s, when the *Lawrence Welk Show* was a Saturday-night ritual. Entertainers Andy Williams, Glen Campbell, Tony Orlando, and other stars who appear on Branson stages sing songs familiar to most people over the age of sixty.

Motel prices start at about $25. You can buy a filling breakfast for less than $3; lunch and dinner prices start at about $4.99. And with tickets generally costing from $17 to $37, you'll find that the shows are less expensive than those in most other parts of the country.

Not only do the theaters present entertainment that's popu-

118

lar with a fair-sized segment of the senior population, many of the theaters, as well as hotels and motels, restaurants, shops, and attractions, offer senior discounts as well. Although stores don't publicize senior discount days, some of them give those discounts when asked. Others have senior discount signs outside their places of business.

Although the amounts of these discounts may not be large, when added to money that can be saved by the discount coupons available to people of all ages, the total savings can be sizable.

BUT WILL *YOU* LIKE BRANSON?

Just because they've reached a certain age doesn't mean that seniors can be lumped in a single group. Like people of all ages, seniors come in a variety of personality types, with varying tastes and interests, not to mention adaptability.

Branson draws more seniors than any other age group—at some times of the year they constitute well over half of the area's tourists. But that doesn't mean it can provide a great vacation for everyone over the age of fifty-five—or of any age, for that matter.

If being surrounded by people who are well coifed and smartly decked out is your idea of a great vacation, you're going to be disappointed with Branson. T-shirts, khakis and baseball caps, casual pants and shorts with knit tops and decorated sweatshirts are about as dressy as it gets. Although food is plentiful, gourmet meals are hard to find. And though there's plenty of entertainment, Branson is not the place to go when you're looking for symphony concerts and high-quality dramatic productions.

Several of the shows reflect the area's Bible Belt, fundamentalist traditions, so you may feel that the overt expressions of religious fervor are excessive. The town is also a favorite reunion spot with servicemen and -women who served in World War II. Catering to these audiences, almost all of the shows include more flag waving than those in other parts of the country.

Even though your favorite ingredients for a great holiday

are missing, if you have a passion for skillfully made crafts or an appreciation for high-caliber musicianship whatever the idiom, you might want to give the Branson area a try. And as we've said, if you love your country Branson is sure to be a shoe-in.

DOING YOUR HOMEWORK

There's no *right* way to see Branson, but chances are you'll have a much better time if you've taken the time to find the way that's most compatible with your travel style. Seniors have the advantage of years of experience and knowing themselves pretty well. Even so, early in the planning process, it's a good idea to ask yourself the following questions and plan your trip in accordance with the answers:

- How much time of each day do I want to spend sight seeing? What attractions do I really want to see?

- What outdoor activities do I like most, and what portion of my vacation do I want to spend pursuing them?

- How many shows do I want to see? Which ones do I think I would like best?

- What kind of accommodations would I prefer—in town or on one of the lakes?

- How important are vacation meals to me?

- How many days and how much money can I comfortably afford to spend?

Seniors who fly to Branson will be able to start off their trips with a discount. Virtually all major U.S. airlines offer two senior options, which are nearly identical. If you're over the age of sixty-two or sixty-five (this varies with the airline), you can pay about $600 for a book of four senior coupons—each valid for a one-way ticket—and use two of them for your Branson trip. Although all four tickets must be purchased within a year of buying the book, you can schedule the travel for any time during the following year.

Seniors can also buy round-trip tickets at a 10 percent discount and take a companion on the same flight for the same price, regardless of the person's age. That means spouse, children, grandchildren, nieces, nephews, younger friends—anyone you choose can travel with you. When you can find a promotional fare that qualifies for the additional 10 percent off, it may be even cheaper than the senior coupons.

Airfare bargains are offered more often on flights between major airports than on those that involve commuter lines. Therefore, people who live near airports used by the airlines such as United, American, Delta, and Northwest, which serve Springfield/Branson with their commuter affiliates, may find they can save a substantial amount of money by flying to Oklahoma City, Kansas City, or some other major airport in the Branson orbit and then driving a rental car to and from Branson. Rental car rates at major airports in the vicinity are also generally lower than those at Springfield.

Spending the extra three or four hours required to drive to Branson and then back again may not make sense for people with two weeks of vacation time each year. And families with kids who go stir-crazy in the car won't want to do it either. Seniors who have more vacation time flexibility, however, can use this technique to their financial advantage, and get in some extra sight-seeing in the bargain.

If you don't want to do any driving at all and are flying into Springfield/Branson Regional Airport without being part of a tour, be prepared for a rather hefty $30 per person for the shuttle ride to Branson ($55 round trip).

TRAVELING WITH FRIENDS

A good many seniors like to travel in the company of friends, but I've heard of more than one longtime friendship that ended in tatters after they traveled together. Chances of friendship survival increase dramatically with the amount of pretrip dialogue among the travelers.

Before you leave home, decide how finances will be handled and who is responsible for various traveling duties such as filling the car with gas, driving, navigating, paying admissions, and other miscellaneous expenses. Many a trip has been spoiled when one person (who always orders the most expensive food) suggests you "split the bill down the middle" or when one member of the group is always too tired to drive. If your trip to and from Branson will require overnight stops, but you don't want to make reservations beforehand, it's always a good plan to determine in advance how you *will* decide when to stop and where to stay. If you wait until everyone's weary from traveling all day, you may have disagreements that could have been avoided.

CHOOSING A COMMERCIAL TOUR

For seniors who can still climb hills like teenagers, Branson's extremely hilly terrain won't present problems. People who can't get around that well and will be traveling alone—or with a non-hill-climbing companion to park the car—should seriously consider taking a commercial tour, since the theaters and attractions have drop-off bus lanes near their entrances. If Branson is high on your "want-to-visit" list, but not on those of your friends, a tour may also be your answer if you don't like solo travel and are willing to put up with a fair amount of regimentation. Commercial tours are also naturals for people who don't want the hassle of taking care of vacation details.

With so many tours available, it can be frustrating trying to find the one that will work best for you. To simplify matters, after you have gathered together all the brochures and other information you can find (see chapter 1 for suggestions about gathering it), zero in on some important tour features that have the potential of making or breaking your trip. You may need a travel agent's help or phone calls to the tour providers to get definite answers to your questions.

- When an itinerary is packed with shows and activities, are any provisions made for people who simply haven't the stamina (or the desire) to participate in all of them?
- Can special dietary or other needs be met?
- Will you be required to carry any luggage?

- If you're taking a motorcoach tour, how often while traveling to and from Branson will your bus make rest room stops?

- If you're traveling by air, will your plane be met at the airport, or will you have to make your own way to Branson?

- How much is a single room supplement? Unless a friend with whom you plan to share a room is going along, you may be happier paying extra so you'll have a room to yourself. Sharing a room with someone you've never met *can* work out, but it can also turn your trip into a disaster.

- Is there any free, unsupervised time built into the itinerary? Two seniors told me that on their tour, they had wanted to browse around the shops near their hotel, but their guide said that the tour company's insurance precluded participants from going anywhere unescorted.

While many seniors are enthusiastic about the age mix they encounter on regular tours, others find that tours designed specifically for seniors better mesh with their preferences and requirements. You'll find dozens of organized tour operators. Among the commercial tour operators specializing in travel for senior singles are **Golden Companions** (P.O. Box 754, Pullman, WA 99163; 208/858-2183) and **Uniworld** (16000 Ventura Boulevard, Encino, CA 91436; 800/858-2183).

Mature Outlook, a Sears operation that specializes in senior travel (800/356-6330), costs $9.95 a year for the enrollee and spouse. It entitles members to 50 percent off published room rates at more than three thousand hotels, motels, and resorts around the world. Membership also brings with it discount coupons on Sears merchandise and a subscription to the organization's magazine.

AARP's Purchase Privilege Program (202/434-2277) provides discounts on lodging, airfare, car and RV rentals, and sight-seeing. Remember, though, that promotions available to the general public can often save you more money than senior discounts that are available, whatever the organization. For further information on tour suppliers, see chapter 1.

Educational Values

Elderhostel offers several classes geared to senior interests in the Branson area. Classes offered in 2001 included Kayak Adventures, which features a first-day practice session and five days with four hours of kayaking per day on Table Rock Lake and Lake Taney-como. While Elderhostelers usually stay in Branson motels, two nights of the kayak course involve camping along Table Rock Lake (program charge: $770).

Ozark Adventures explores the culture, history, and geology of the Ozarks. Participants learn about the hardships that the pioneers and early settlers suffered when they lived in log cabins and farmed with mules. The Civil War and its influence and the development of area rivers are also discussed in these five-day sessions. A Branson excursion to see and hear nationally recognized musicians playing the old-time tunes is also part of the course, whose instructors include some of the Ozark's finest writers, folklorists, musicians, and artisans.

The Ozarks "Spring" to Life captures the essence of the Ozark springtime, with its trees bursting with new leaves and its wildflowers and plants emerging on the hillsides. Herbal remedies, culture, history, and other subjects similar to those pursued in Ozark Adventures are the focus of this five-day course. The Ozarks Adventures and the Ozarks "Spring" to Life courses each cost $490.

Branson Show Biz centers around the history and development of the Ozarks region and the folk traditions that have influenced the Branson formula of entertainment. It reviews the tourism industry with emphasis on "out-of-market" and "intercept" marketing as well as analyzing cutting-edge show business production elements such as lighting, acoustics and sound control, scenery, and costuming. Course participants also tour area theaters and attend several productions. Professionals working in the Branson entertainment industry assist with the instruction. The program fee is $495.

A course called the Heritage of Country Music in Branson: Cultural Changes in Boom Town Branson made its debut in the winter 2002 Elderhostel catalog. The course traces the area's history from "barn-jammin' " days to twenty-first-century glitz in order to learn how the area became the "new music capital of the world." The rugged life of the Ozark settlers, the 1880 and 1992 booms, and major changes in the region are among the topics covered. Classroom time is augmented by field trips, shows, and conversations with live performers. Cost of the seven-day course is $531 per person with a double occupancy room and $631 per person with a single room.

SENIOR SAVINGS

Savvy seniors who want to save money will find opportunities in abundance. Not only are there the coupons available to people of all ages, which are described in the preceding chapters, but there are also dozens of deals specifically for seniors.

Check the restaurants' menus and you'll see that a good many of them have sections devoted to senior specials. In many restaurants these specials include smaller portions of dishes that are also listed on the main menu. Some Branson restaurants have special senior and children's meals listed together, with headings such as "for people under ten and over sixty." Senior specials may be available only during certain hours, but more often they're offered whenever the restaurant is open.

Always inquire about senior discounts when booking rooms in hotels and motels. Almost every hostelry gives discounts to members of the American Association of Retired Persons (AARP) and other senior groups. Some properties even offer additional discounts in their competition for the senior trade. Of course, you'll want to compare those rates with any packages the hotel or motel may be offering to see which will be the better deal for you.

Many Branson theaters have a range of special fares for seniors, so before you pay for any tickets, find out what savings they have to offer.

PRACTICAL PACKING

When you travel by airline or are part of a motorcoach tour you're usually allowed two pieces of luggage and one carry-on bag. Unless you plan to stay in Branson for an extended period of time, your life will be less complicated if you bring along your carry-on and only one bag. Since attire is casual, you simply won't need a lot of clothes for dressing up: A couple of pairs of slacks or khakis and a few shirts or knit tops will keep you looking appropriately dressed. Remember, though, to bring along a sweater to wear when the weather's cool or the

It's a Nice Place to Visit, But . . .

During the past couple of decades, hundreds of retirees have decided that they want to live in the Branson area. In fact, seniors make up more than 43 percent of the area's population. Many of them are retired military people who spent tours of duty in Missouri or surrounding states and discovered the region's lakeside living.

Among the reasons people choose the Branson area, in addition to the quality of life, is that the average home price is $107,000, whereas the national average is $142,500. In many cases, houses and condominiums on golf courses cost half of what they do in other resort areas. It's possible to buy condos overlooking Table Rock Lake for less than $100,000. And although there are multimillion-dollar lakeside estates and some homes in the new subdivisions cost more than half a million dollars, many new-home prices are less than $200,000.

Other advantages are that revenue from tourism keeps city taxes low, and the cost of living is 6 percent below the national average. There are also plenty of job opportunities for people who find that retirement is less exciting than they had imagined. Full- or part-time jobs working in theater box offices or ushering, greeting customers at discount stores like Kmart, and demonstrating crafts at theme parks are among the possibilities. And since Branson's tourism is seasonal, it's possible to work and still have lots of days off for golf and other leisure time activities.

People who are visiting Branson with the thought of choosing it for their retirement home will want to visit the chamber of commerce to obtain a relocation packet that contains extensive information on real estate, city government, attractions, events, medical services, and other facilities.

air-conditioning is turned on high (and a hat and sunscreen for protection from ultraviolet rays). I've found that when traveling, the less encumbered I am with possessions, the more time I have to spend doing what I want to do.

Carry any medications you need to take regularly in your hand luggage, and include copies of the prescriptions with other papers you take along. When your medications include any that require refrigeration, notify hotel personnel (or the tour company) in advance so that you can have the use of a small refrigerator. Should you need medical care while in Branson, it's available at the Skaggs Community Health Center (North Business Highway 65 and Skaggs Road; 417/335-7000).

11

Day Trips

Not only are there shows and attractions by the score in Branson, but it's also a great day-trippers' base of operations. In fact, there are so many possibilities for excursions that we've confined this chapter to those that are no more than an hour and a half away by car.

SILVER DOLLAR CITY

Let me point out right now that I am not a theme park fan. Cute little figures that sing in cute little voices leave me yawning. White-knuckle rides and the accompanying shrieks give me the screaming meemies.

But Silver Dollar City, nine miles west of Branson on Indian Point Road (800/831-4FUN), is not that kind of theme park. A day is barely long enough to visit the more than fifty old-time crafts shops, tour the cave, take the rides (actually, there are a few of the white-knuckle variety), and watch the entertainment that goes on virtually nonstop at various venues on the grounds.

Buildings of rough gray and tan planking line the broad paths. A windmill, a gazebo, barrels, and other props contribute to the old-time atmosphere without seeming hokey. The park is especially attractive in autumn, when tastefully arranged pumpkins, scarecrows, and beribboned cornstalks provide additional splashes of color to the fall foliage.

In one of the rustic buildings, you'll find a broom maker, fashioning everything from hearth brooms to those with which you might sweep out the garage. In another, glassblowers work at red-hot furnaces to produce paperweights, intricately decorated vases, and other one-of-a-kind items. One hundred full-time crafters are part of Silver Dollar City's twelve-hundred-member staff.

Wood-carvers, basket weavers, lye soap and candle makers, copper workers, printers, quilters, and scrimshaw carvers demonstate their crafts and answer any questions visitors may have. And if you want to buy their wares, you'll find them displayed in the shops.

These old-time crafts are especially interesting because they give visitors an idea of how hard life was in bygone days. Men with broadaxes hew pine timbers for a log cabin; a Missouri mule walks in circles to propel the press that crushes juice from sorghum cane.

Another mule powers the "walk-around" hay baler, and a waterwheel supplies the power that operates a massive drop forge hammer and screw press that produce souvenir coins. A bodger makes bentwood Windsor chairs.

When it's time to take a rest—and Silver Dollar City's hilly terrain may have you puffing a bit—you'll find lots of benches surrounding the park's entertainment areas. That entertainment ranges from melodrama to all sorts of music. The 2001 daily entertainment lineup included a baker's dozen different acts performing at various venues on the Silver Dollar City grounds.

Among them, the Cajun connection band presented thirty minutes of music and dancing four times a day at the **Dockside Theatre,** while Australia's yodeling cowboy, Wayne Horsburgh, performed five times daily on the gazebo stage. Gospel singers, Native American dancers, banjo pickers, and gunslingers appeared at the **Opera House Theatre, Carousel Barn, Silver Dollar Saloon, Boatworks Theatre, Riverfront Playhouse,** and **Frisco Barn.** During festivals, additional musicians and other entertainers join the regular Silver Dollar City performers.

Providing less structured entertainment, storytellers keep

kids and grown-ups enthralled with their yarns. Street per-formers stroll the theme park's paths, singing and making the crowds laugh. Each evening, a country western show called Sundown Jubilee bursts with toe-tapping enthusiasm from the stage of the three thousand-seat Echo Hollow Amphitheatre. It's a show that's suitable for the whole family.

The most exciting—and usually the most crowded—time to visit Silver Dollar City is during the **National Crafts Festival,** held each year from mid-September through October. Crafts, from cornshuckery to cooperage (barrel making), are demonstrated by almost one hundred artisans. Since the working participants in the festival can come by invitation only, the items they produce are the cream of the craftworkers' crop.

Among the most attractive items produced for sale at the 2001 festival were smartly styled quilted jackets and little girls' bonnets decorated with English embroidery by Jennifer Sharpe. At a nearby stall, Julie Topolinski demonstrated Scandinavian rug making, while in the gazebo area, members of the Schrock family showed the crowds how to make sorghum from cane sugar stalks.

Other special events held throughout the year are **World-Fest** (the first week in April through the first week in May), featuring entertainers and artisans from countries around the globe; the **Great American Music Festival,** with entertainers such as Peter, Paul & Mary (mid-May through the first week in June); **National Children's Festival,** a marathon of hands-on activities and entertainment especially designed for young-sters (mid-June through late August); and **Old Time Christmas** (early November to December 23).

The best way to enjoy Silver Dollar City is to ignore time constraints. And forget about counting calories, since places like **Flossie's Fried Fancies, Hannah's Ice Cream Palace,** and **Berries and Cream** sell snacks too tempting to resist. My fa-vorites are the funnel cakes sprinkled with powdered sugar ($2.59). When smothered with blackberry, peach, wild cherry, or cinnamon apple topping, the funnel cakes cost $4.19.

Operating days and hours at Silver Dollar City vary throughout the year, but from mid-May through the first two-thirds of August, the park is open daily from 9:30 A.M. to 7 P.M. One-day admission for ages twelve and over is $36.05; seniors over fifty-five, $33.90; children four through eleven, $24.35. It's also possible to buy tickets at 3 P.M. that are good for the rest of the day plus the next day at no extra charge. Another deal allows ticket holders to spend a full day at Silver Dollar City and then, upon leaving, get tickets for the next day for only $12. A season pass costs $62.55. During November and December, when the rides are not in operation, tickets cost $30.75, $19.10, and $28.60. Several discount coupons for Silver Dollar City, including one for $1 off the Mill Restaurant breakfast buffet, are available in various entertainment publications. For more information, phone 800/952-6626 or go to www.silverdollarcity.com.

BRANSON USA THEME PARK

Although located at the junction of Missouri Highways 76 and 376 at the edge of central Branson, we have included Branson USA amusement park (1838 Highway 76; 417/335-2396) as an excursion rather than an attraction. The reason is this: To our way of thinking, families who pony up the major money required for unlimited ride tickets (adults and children ten years and older, $19.95; children ages three through nine, $11.95) will want to get their money's worth by turning the experience into an all-day excursion. Tickets bought after eight in the evening are good for the entire next day as well. So in summer and during November and December—when the park stays open until midnight—people who want to get the utmost from unlimited ride tickets buy them at 8:01 P.M. They use the tickets until closing time, then spend the next day on the rides.

Even so, it may be impossible to experience every one of the thirty midway rides, since lines of people waiting to go on the most popular ones, like the Wind Storm Roller Coaster, can be long. The Flying Dragon Wagon, Free-Fall, Zyklon Coaster, and Paratrooper are other popular rides.For the little ones, rides include Big Chief ChooChoo, the Big Truck, and a carousel. Go-cart tracks, bumper cars, and a miniature golf course are other kid pleasers.

Silver Dollar City's Craft College

For people who want to learn how to make furniture, weave baskets from oak strips, dip candles, or hammer metal, classes at Silver Dollar City's Craft College may be the answer. Students apprentice with talented master craftspeople to learn such skills as glassblowing, basket weaving, Damascus knife making, chair weaving, candle making and carving, scrimshanding, leather working, porcelain doll making, and sandcasting. There's wood carving, too, with classes including general basics, relief carving, hillbilly caricatures, Native American busts, Santas, and chip carving.

Classes run from one to four days; Craft College Seminars, three to five days long, are held annually. The latter include specialized classes for beginners as well as advanced crafters. For example, some of the best weavers in the country are brought in to participate in the basket-making seminar, and the wood-carving seminars include two dozen or more wood-carving classes. For more information on classes and seminars, call 417/338-8232.

People who don't have enough time for a class or seminar can participate in the Craftsman for a Day program. Outfitted in period costume by the Silver Dollar City costume shop, apprentice blacksmiths, knife makers, basket makers, tintype photographers, bakers, lye soap makers, leather crafters, and taffy makers spend the day working with a skilled craftsperson. At the end of the day, each apprentice takes home a finished craft or product and receives a tintype photos of him- or herself at work. For more information, phone 800/695-1353.

Included in the admission price are two shows. The afternoon production is called Today's Country and begins at 1 P.M. The Magnificent 7 Show, which starts at 7 P.M., stars a fifteen-year-old named Amanda Haffecke, who does everything from yodeling to singing "Somewhere Over the Rainbow" and "Tomorrow."

Since admission to the Branson USA grounds and parking are free, it's possible to save considerable money if the adults in the party aren't interested in taking the rides or seeing the shows. Another way to reduce costs is to look for the discount tickets allowing $5 off an adult's and $2 off a child's price. These coupons are small and printed on sheets with a host of other coupons, so you will need to look carefully to spot them.

SHEPHERD OF THE HILLS HOMESTEAD

Totally different from Silver Dollar City and Branson USA is Branson's theme park with the oldest roots—Shepherd of the Hills Homestead (5586 West Highway 76; 417/334-4191). Two miles west of Branson (a walkway under the highway leads to the park's entrance), the Homestead—where novelist Harold Bell Wright stayed with homesteaders John and Anna Ross—was bought by Lizzie McDaniel in 1923 after the Rosses had died. Daughter of a Springfield banker, McDaniel restored the cabin, and the first dramatizations of Wright's *Shepherd of the Hills* were presented on the lawn.

After McDaniel's death, Dr. Bruce and Mary Trimble acquired the property in 1946 and added a number of attractions. Under the Trimble ownership, performances of *Shepherd of the Hills* began in 1960 and became the country's leading outdoor performance of the time. Twenty-five years later, the property was sold to Gary Snadon, who had portrayed the villain in the play during the late 1960s.

In 1997, the ninety-member cast celebrated the show's five thousandth performance. The current production—in addition to the human cast—features thirty-two live horses, twenty-eight single-action Ruger revolvers, and twenty-two double-barreled shotguns. The show is presented nightly April through October, except when it's raining.

During the day at Shepherd of the Hills Homestead, guided jeep tours take visitors back in Ozark history to the days of circuit-riding preachers and the vigilantes-turned-bad-guys known as the Bald Knobbers. Among the stops on the tour is Old Matt's cabin (home of the main characters in the novel and designated a National Historic Landmark). Lizzie McDaniel's home, a still for making moonshine, sawmill, blacksmith shop, gristmill, and wheelwright are other places of interest on the property.

The park's most imposing feature is its 230-foot-tall Inspiration Tower, which weighs three million pounds. The enclosed observation deck is surrounded by four thousand four hundred square feet of glass. There's also an open-air observation deck with telescopes for close-up views, though there's not a great deal more to see than the panorama of trees and hills. Tickets to the tower, when not bought as part of a package, cost $5. (For a million-dollar view that's absolutely free, see chapter 5, Shopping and Souvenirs).

At various locations throughout the Homestead, craftspeople demonstrate their skills and performers present live entertainment. There's Aunt Mollie's buffet-style restaurant, too, offering fried chicken, mashed potatoes, string beans, and hot breads.

Annual events at the Homestead include **Pioneer Days** in May, the weeklong summer **Bluegrass Festival, Cruisin' Branson Lights Automotive Festival** (classic and custom vehicles plus hot rods) in August, and the **Fall Harvest Festival**. The latter event, which is free to the public, features dozens of crafters demonstrating their skills, which range from wheat weaving and leather work to candle making and wood painting.

The Homestead is open daily from late April through Labor Day from 9 A.M. to 5 P.M. Admission to the site is free. A combination ticket—which includes the jeep tour, a visit to Inspiration Tower, and admission to the play—costs $27 for adults; $12 for children ages four through sixteen). Individual attraction tickets for adults cost $5 for the tower ($2 for children) and $21 for the play ($10).

SPRINGFIELD

About thirty-five miles due north of Branson, Springfield, Missouri, is a destination in its own right. With three lakes nearby, it's a recreation center. Bass Country Antique Mall (1832 South Campbell Street) features more than a hundred dealers; the Commercial Street Historical District is also an antiques and vintage clothing shop locale. There are historic buildings, too, including Christ Episcopal Church, with stained-glass windows and Gothic ecclesiastical architecture.

The biggest tourist draw in Springfield, however, is **Bass Pro Shops Outdoor World** (1935 South Campbell Street; 417/887-7334), which features a 140,000-gallon game fish aquarium, a 30,000-gallon saltwater aquarium, a four-story waterfall, and a trout pond. There are also a hunting museum and a wildlife art gallery on the premises. It's open Monday through Saturday, 7 A.M. to 10 P.M.; Sunday, 9 A.M. to 6 P.M. There's an admission charge for the museum, but the other attractions are free.

Since the primary purpose of the operation is to sell hunting, fishing, and camping gear, it's a great shopping destination for people interested in these pursuits. Within the cavernous store you can find everything from fishing weights to thermal underwear. There's also a huge area of the complex devoted to boats, motors, and recreational vehicle sales.

At a counter near the trout pond, you can sign up for a Bass Pro Shops Visa Card and get a free Bass Pro Shops T-shirt. The credit card, for which there's no annual fee, rewards cardholders with certificates redeemable for any Bass Pro Shops, Red Head, or Offshore Angler merchandise (1 percent of the price of purchases charged on the card).

Nature lovers won't want to miss **Springfield Conservation Nature Center** (4600 Chrisman Avenue; Highway 60W exit off Highway 65; 417/888-4237), eighty acres along Lake Springfield with about three miles of trails. Deer, raccoons, and other wildlife live in the forests and fields. Turtles sun themselves on the creek banks. You can also look at natural history exhibits as well as purchase your hunting and fishing permits at the preserve's visitor center.

Springfield National Cemetery (1702 East Seminole Street; 417/881-9499) is the final resting place for both Union and Confederate soldiers, along with veterans of all the U.S. wars. The headstones of the five Medal of Honor recipients buried in the cemetery are engraved in gold.

The **Missouri Sports Hall of Fame** (5051 Highland Springs Boulevard; 417/889-3100) honors the most memorable of Missouri teams and players. Would-be sportscasters and big-leaguers will enjoy the interactive broadcast booth and the pitching cage, which dispenses balls at one-hundred-plus miles per hour. Open Monday through Saturday, 10 A.M. to 4 P.M.; Sunday noon to 4 P.M. Admission is $5 for adults, $4 for seniors, and $3 for ages six through fifteen. There's also a family rate of $14.

Families with youngsters will want to spend some time at **Discovery Center** (438 St. Louis Street; 417/862-9910). Among the interactive displays, there's a pint-sized town where visitors can anchor news broadcasts, write articles for the newspaper, and withdraw play money at the bank. Open Wednesday through Friday and Sunday, 1 to 5 P.M.; Saturday, 10 A.M. to 5 P.M. Admission is $5 for people over twelve years, $4 for seniors, and $3 for children ages three through twelve.

On display at **Dickerson Park Zoo** (3043 North Fort Avenue; 417/833-1570) are about 150 species of animals and birds—including bald eagles. It's open daily April through September from 9 A.M. to 5 P.M; abbreviated hours the rest of the year. Admission is $4 for adults, $3.25 for people over sixty-five, and $2.50 for ages three through twelve. Animal fanciers should also check out the Exotic Animal Paradise (twelve miles east of Springfield on I-44; 417/859-2159), where a nine-and-a-half-mile paved road takes visitors past a variety of wild animals and rare birds—about three thousand in all. There's also a Safari Center on the grounds, which is home to monkeys and exotic birds. Open daily, 8 A.M. to 7 P.M. Admission runs $9.99 for adults, $8.99 for people over fifty-four years, and $5.99 for children ages three through eleven.

ANTIQUE HUNTER'S HUNTING GROUNDS

Since the Ozarks have long been known for their crafts, it's not surprising that the most gratifying treasures in antiques stores are, more often than not, the crafts of bygone days: handmade tools, hand-blocked quilts, chenille bedspreads made for the 1930s tourist trade, primitive musical instruments. There also are the Victorian-era antiques—proud possessions of the mountain folk who had done well enough financially to buy cranberry glass pickle casters from the Sears Roebuck catalog; cut-glass candy dishes that in the early twentieth century were given as grocery store premiums.

The best single place in the Branson area to find antiques, experts say, is in the town of **Ozark,** about twenty-seven miles north of Branson on U.S. Highway 65. The largest concentration of shops is at **Finley River Park Center** (southwest corner at the junction of Highways 65 and 14; turn left off Highway 14 just east of the Phillips 66 station). **Maine Streete Mall Antiques** (1994 Evangel Street, Ozark; 417/581-2575), the first of the antiques operations at the Finley River Park, opened in 1988. Now the mall has a roster of 130 dealers from eight states. Needless to say, the array of merchandise is eclectic— everything from paper valentines and cut-glass sugar bowls to wooden spoons and metal garden trellises. The mall is at its liveliest on the Memorial Day and Labor Day weekends when it sponsors an outdoor flea fest, with outdoor stalls adding to the items for sale inside.

Antique Emporium (Finley River Park complex, 1702 West Boat Street, Ozark; 417/581-5555), with more than a hundred vendors' booths, is the place you're most likely to find old tools, fishing tackle, and boat motors. There's also quite a selection of old golf clubs, bags, and such.

Ozark Antiques (200 South 20th Street, Ozark; 417/581-5233) specializes in collectibles, most of them from the 1930s and 1940s, including World War II mementos. With more than two hundred dealers, this gigantic operation is filled with old Coke machines, tractor seats, metal bedsteads, bright red hand pumps, vintage tricycles, pottery, coins, railroad memorabilia, and just about everything else.

Pine Merchant Inc. (140 North 20th Street; 417/581-7333) is several cuts above the other antiques shops in both appearance and general quality of its merchandise. A family-owned business, about 80 percent of Pine Merchant's merchandise is antique furniture and home furnishings; the rest is composed of reproductions. The antiques are primarily imported from Hungary, Belgium, Holland, Germany, England, France, and other European countries. The Café at the back of the store serves lunch, with quiche, soup, salads, and desserts on its menu.

Crossroads Antique Mall (2004 West Evangel Street, Ozark; 417/581-0428) is another of the Finley River Park enterprises, with more than sixty antiques dealers involved in the operation. There are also a couple of collectibles shops in the complex.

Go east of Finley River Park on Missouri Highway 14 for about a mile, and you'll find another cluster of antiques stores and flea markets. They're a rather motley group, but they're the sort of shops that yield true bargains to people who know their antiques and take the time to look for them.

Riverview Antique Center (909 West Jackson Street, Ozark; 417/581-4426) has an extensive collection of books and price guides on hand, so if you don't know what the item you're looking at is—or what it's worth—you can thumb through the resource materials until you find the answer. Riverview has a good selection of tools and also some nifty items from the 1920s among its extensive stock of collectibles.

Across the parking lot, **Ozark Flea Market's** (417/581-8544) inventory ranges from a 1930s doll buggy and a bright red Radio Flyer wagon to a metal Flying A service station sign. At the very rear of the complex there's a pawn shop and **Riverview Flea Mart,** the most organized of the stores. Farther along Missouri Highway 14, **Spring Creek Antiques and Tea Room** (107 South 3rd Street; 417/581-5914) features one of the nicest selections of antiques in the area.

For people who love to eat, the best part of an antiques excursion to Ozark may well be having lunch or dinner at **Lambert's** (four miles north on Highway 65; 1800 West Highway J; 417/581-5914). Operated by the same family since it opened in 1942, the restaurant's interior is a fantasy of flags, planes, and paper balloons hanging from the ceilings and board walls above the booths completely covered with license plates, old-time advertisements, pictures, and signs.

Food portions are enormous, and every entrée—whether it's hog jowl (it tastes rather like bacon) or Polish sausage and kraut (both $7.99); barbecue pork steak or chicken and dumplings ($9.99); or fried catfish fillets ($12.99)—comes with a choice of two vegetables (there are eighteen items from which to choose), thrown rolls (waiters throw them to diners), and "pass-arounds." Those include macaroni and tomatoes, fried okra, black-eyed peas, and fried potatoes. According to one waiter, "Only teenagers and construction workers are able to eat everything on their plates."

EUREKA SPRINGS

About sixty miles southwest of Branson in Arkansas, Eureka Springs has been a travelers' destination since the mid-1800s, when a clinic was established there and people came from miles around to "take the waters." As the spas diminished in importance, tourists found additional reasons to visit the little town.

It's a charmer, spilling down from the hills to a canyon just wide enough for Main Street and a few blocks of buildings dating from the 1880s. They mostly contain tourist-oriented businesses now—old-time photo studios, antiques dealers, a fudge shop.

The best time to arrive is in early morning before the crowds, perhaps starting off the day's adventures with breakfast at the **Main Street Café** (39 South Main Street; 501/253-7374). Originally a saloon in the late nineteenth century, it has been a restaurant for some forty years. And though it has been gussied up somewhat for the tourist trade, with framed watercolors hanging on the white walls above the wainscoting, there's still a locals table in the back where men wearing caps advertising motor oil and seed companies have their morning coffee.

Today more than a dozen attractions (many of them biblical-themed), crafts and antiques shopping, and recreational facilities at surrounding lakes combine to make the area one of the most popular in the region. Elegant turn-of-the-twentieth-century homes are featured in self-guided tours, with brochures available at the **chamber of commerce** (81 Kings Highway; 800/6-EUREKA). There's also a re-created early-nineteenth-century town called **Abundant Memories Heritage Village**, two and a half miles north of Eureka Springs (501/253-6764), which includes twenty-six furnished shops, offices, houses, and other buildings. Artisans producing different crafts and performances at the **Historama Theatre** add to the experience. Open daily, 9:30 A.M. to 4:30 P.M., May 1 to early November; admission is $8 for adults, $4.50 for ages twelve through seventeen, $3.50 for ages five through eleven. Telephone 501/ 253-3764.

Among the religious attractions is **The Great Passion Play,** presented under the stars in an amphitheater three miles east of town (800/882-7529 or 501/253-9200); ticket prices are $15.25 for adults, $7.50 for ages four through eleven. Showtimes and days vary with the seasons.

Three attractions can be visited by using the same ticket. The **Bible Museum** (Smith Memorial Chapel, four and a half miles northeast of town; 501/253-8559) contains more than six thousand Bibles in 625 languages and dialects. **New Holy Land Tour** (three miles east of Eureka Springs; 501/253-9200) is a guided two-hour bus tour through a fifty-acre area that recreates biblical scenes such as the inn at Bethlehem and a walk with Peter around the Sea of Galilee. The third attraction, **Sacred Arts Center** (three-plus miles northeast of Eureka Springs), contains more than a thousand pieces of biblical art in media including marble, needlepoint, and oil paints. Tickets to the three attractions cost $7.50 for adults, $3.75 for ages four through eleven.

Belle of the Ozarks at **Starkey Park** (four miles from town; 800/552-3803 or 501/253-6200) takes passengers along the shores of Beaver Lake. Sights along the way include Beaver Dam, White House Bluffs, and the two hundred-acre game preserve. From Memorial Day weekend to Labor Day, cruises leave Thursday through Tuesday at 11 A.M., 1, 3, and 7 P.M. The fare is $12 for adults, $6 for ages two through twelve.

Or you might choose to ride the **Eureka Springs and North Arkansas Railway.** The forty-five-minute narrated rides on a restored steam train leave from the original depot at 299 North Main Street (501/253-9623 or 253-9677). Lunch and dinner trips are available, too. Departures from April through October leave on the hour Monday through Saturday, 10 A.M. to 4 P.M. Fare is $8 for adults, $4 for ages four through ten. Dinner is $24.95 per adult. Lunch costs $14.95 for adults, $8.45 for children under eight years (reservations are required for trips when meals are served).

Instead of spending money on any of the above attractions,

you might catch a trolley at the downtown station or at the **Eureka Springs Visitors Center** (137 West Van Buren; 501/253-8737). At the center, you'll be able to load up on discount coupons and a free trolley map. The trolleys run seven days a week beginning at 9 A.M. They stop operating at 5, 6, or 8 P.M., depending on the season. An all-day pass costs $3.50.

The most popular route (marked in red on the map) follows the historic loop through downtown's shopping area and one of the town's older residential districts. The blue route travels between the downtown trolley depot and the *Great Passion Play* grounds, while the green route goes between the visitor center and the north edge of town, stopping at the North Arkansas Railway Station.

The purple route goes between downtown and the **Razorback Observation Tower,** which is a short walk from **Thorncrown Chapel** (12968 West Highway 62; 501/253-7401), one of Eureka Springs's most popular attractions. The chapel, reaching forty-eight feet into the sky, is constructed in a latticelike style with wood strips and glass panes, which virtually makes the building one with the outdoors.

Also on the purple line is **Wings** (111 Van Buren; 417/253-8825), a Victorian home that's decorated for Christmas year-round. Exotic birds in aviaries and an almost life-sized Italian nativity are also on display.

Since all of the central portion of Eureka Springs has been designated a National Historic District, you might also want to wander around exploring the late-nineteenth-century architecture. A forty-two-page brochure published by the Eureka Preservation Society contains maps for six separate walking tours and descriptions of sites along the way. It's available at both the **Eureka Springs Historical Museum** (95 South Main Street: 501/253-9417) and at the visitor center.

If you would like to walk some more, go to **Lake Leatherwood** on the northwest end of town where three major trails—**Miner's Rock Trail** (1.3 miles), **Beacham Trail** (3.8 miles around the lake), and **Fuller Trail** (1.1 miles)—are, like the downtown routes, maintained by the parks and recreation department.

MOUNTAIN VIEW

The **Ozark Folk Center** is the main attraction in this little Arkansas town about eighty-two miles southeast of Branson on Arkansas Highway 382 (870/269-3139). The center, which actually is about two and a half miles north of Mountain View, focuses on crafts, music, and dance. It's especially interesting when special events such as the annual **Arkansas Folk Festival,** the **Southern Regional Mountain** and **Hammer Dulcimer Workshop and Contest** (April), the **Arkansas Old-Time Fiddlers Association State Championship Competition** (mid-September), and the **Fall Harvest Festival** (October) take place. For more information, telephone 870/269-3851. From April through October, craft demonstrations are featured daily from 10 A.M. to 5 P.M. Musical performances are presented in the auditorium Monday through Saturday at 7:30 P.M. from mid-April through October. Admission to the craft area is $7.50 for adults, $5 for children. The family rate is $17.75. The same admissions are charged for musical performances. Combination crafts and musical program tickets cost $13.25 for adults, $7.25 for ages six through twelve, the family price is $31.75. There's also an old mill in the town of Mountain View (306 West Main Street; 870/269-5337), where the original kerosene motor still provides power for the gristmill.

SOUTH SHORE, BULL SHOALS LAKE

When you want to take a break from Branson bustle and hustle, you won't have to go far to Bull Shoals Lake. Just head south on U.S. Highway 65 to the junction with Arkansas Highway 14 that's one mile south of the Arkansas state line. Turn left onto Highway 14, and the first town you'll drive through is **Omaha** (population 101), home of **Roberson Farm Market.**

At the market, counters are piled high with bags of cashews, pistachios, peanuts, and black walnuts; apples of half a dozen varieties, trail mix, and candy. Shelves brim with jars of pickled okra, canned green tomato pickles, chow chow, piccalilli, and black bean salsa. There are countless bottles and cans of sorghum molasses; jars of fig spread and strawberry preserves; bottles of peach, blueberry, and black walnut syrup.

Stalactites and Stalagmites

Throughout the Branson region are caves galore—some of them open to the public. While it's not a good idea to go spelunking (exploring caves) on your own unless you've had instruction and are experienced, the commercially run caves are safe, if you follow the guides' instructions and don't go wandering off on your own.

Among the major caves in the area are **Fantastic Caverns,** four and a half miles northwest of Springfield and one of Missouri's largest. No walking is necessary in this cave: A forty-five-minute tram tour takes passengers on the one-mile ride through the electrically lighted cavern. The formations include giant pillars of stone, tiny cave pearls, and delicate soda straws as well as the usual stalactites and stalagmites. Open daily from 8 A.M. to dusk, admission is $14.50 for adults and $7.95 for people ages six through twelve. Phone 417/833-2010 for information.

Onyx Cave, three miles east of Eureka Springs, Arkansas, offers thirty-minute self-guiding tours with taped narration. Picnicking is permitted at the park, which is open daily from 8:30 A.M. to 6:30 P.M., May through September (shorter hours during other times of the year; 501/253-9321). Admission is $3.75 for adults, $1.95 for ages four through thirteen.

Blanchard Springs Caverns, fifteen miles northwest of Mountain View on Arkansas Highway 14, offers guided tours. The half-mile Dripstone Trail tour explores the upper level of the cave and lasts one hour. The 1.2-mile Discovery Trail tour follows water-carved passages to the cavern's middle level. This second tour involves lots of step climbing and takes about two hours. Both tours leave every hour between 9 A.M. and 6 P.M. daily from Memorial Day weekend through Labor Day. There is a Dripstone Trail tour during the rest of the year (888/757-2246 or 870/757-2211). Tours cost $9 for adults and $5 for ages six through fifteen.

Talking Rocks Cavern, about fifteen miles northwest of Branson (turn left off Highway 76 at the junction with Highway 13 and go to Talking Rocks Road; 800/600-CAVE or 417/272-3366; www.talking rockscavern.com), provides fifty-minute tours that start approximately every thirty minutes most of the year (adults, $11.95; children five through twelve, $5.95; a $1 discount ticket on merchandise purchased at the cave is in the *TravelHost* brochures). The spectacular cave—considered one of the state's most beautiful—is within a four hundred-acre nature preserve. There are nature trails and picnic areas on the grounds. It's also possible to take a **Wild Cave Tour,** accompanied by two experienced cave guides, into one of the ten caves on the Talking Rocks Cavern grounds. Called Indian Creek, it's the third longest cave that has been discovered to date in Missouri and has no lights or graded paths with handrails. Cost of the tour is $250 for four people, with $50 for each additional person. Helmets with lights—plus a fresh set of lights—are available for rent ($10). Talking Rock Cavern and grounds are open daily June through August, 9 A.M. to 7 P.M. The attraction is open the rest of the year Tuesday through Friday, from 9:30 A.M to 5 P.M.

Tours of **Bull Shoals Caverns** in Mountain Village 1890 last forty-five-minutes and are offered daily from 9 A.M. to 6 P.M., mid-May through Labor Day and at various times throughout other parts of the year. The tour costs $8 for adults, $6 for ages six through eleven. A combination admission to the Mountain Village 1890 and the caverns costs $12 for adults and $9 for children. Other area caves include Cosmic Cavern, billed as "Arkansas' most beautifully decorated show cave" (midway between Branson and Eureka Springs), and Marvel Cave, underneath Silver Dollar City.

Formed some 350 million years ago, the caves are quite cool (usually in the fifties), and the atmosphere is damp. Floors tend to be wet and are often somewhat slippery. Remember to wear a jacket, long pants, and shoes with good traction. If you're wearing shorts and sandals, postpone the excursion for later.

A few miles beyond Omaha, Arkansas Highway 28 leads to **Tucker Hollow Park,** a low-key recreational center with three lake resorts as well as camping facilities and a boat launch. Farther along Arkansas Highway 14, at its junction with Arkansas Highways 7 and 268, you can turn off to **Diamond City** (population 601), where there's a boat marina and a golf course surrounded by peaceful countryside.

Instead of going to Diamond City, by taking a combination of Arkansas Highway 268, County Road 259, and Arkansas Highway 125, you'll arrive at the town of **Peel** and the **Peel ferry,** the last boat remaining in the Arkansas State Highway Department ferry system. The ferry makes the trip across the lake every twenty minutes (it operates only during daylight hours), and it's free. To return to Branson, either retrace your route or proceed on Highway 125 to U.S. Highway 160 and go west.

WHITEWATER THRILLS

Though you will have to drive about an hour and a half east of Branson, if you're fond of whitewater rafting, you can find challenging rapids on the north fork of the **White River. North Fork Outfitters** (junction of Highways 181 and CC West, Dora; 417/261-2259) offer a variety of one-day trips lasting from four and a half to seven hours on rubber rafts with experienced guides.

It's also possible to rent canoes, rafts, and kayaks for do-it-yourself trips. Canoe rentals cost $35 if you're renting only one, with ever-decreasing amounts depending on the quantity rented by your party—rent nine and they're $25 each. Rubber rafts rent for $60 a day, kayaks for $20. Life jackets are a must.

COMMERCIAL TOURS

If you are without a car—or would rather leave the driving to someone else—you'll find that a few commercial tours are available.

A Slice of the Ozarks is a three-hour narrated tour of Branson and the surrounding lakes area. It includes sights along Country Music Boulevard, old downtown Branson, the historic community of Hollister, College of the Ozarks, the Scenic Overlook, and Table Rock Dam. At tour's end, participants stop at a theater where they're greeted by a celebrity, have their photos taken, and receive an autographed souvenir. The Branson Gray Line (3050 Green Mountain Drive; 417/334-5463) tour is offered Monday, Thursday, and Saturday at 9 A.M. ($20 per person).

The Antique and Craft Road Show takes participants on a seven-hour circuit through the back roads of the Ozarks looking for treasures from the past and handmade crafts. Offered on Wednesday only, the tour costs $40 per person. Other Gray Line tours include a six-hour excursion to Eureka Springs, Arkansas, which allows time for browsing the boutiques and galleries ($40), and a three-hour **Festival of Lights** holiday tour, which costs $20 per person.

12

For More Information

The Branson scene is continually changing. And expanding. Hotels, motels, and theaters go quickly from the drawing board to construction. New attractions and shopping malls spring up. Restaurants open, and sometimes close. Fortunately, several sources of information remain the same. These are the sources you should contact while you're planning your trip and after you arrive in town.

MAKING PLANS

The more information you have, the easier trip planning becomes, and the more savings you're ultimately able to make. Free publications include:

Best Read Guide
P.O. Box 6009
Branson, MO 65615
417/336-7323
www.bestreadguide.com/branson/

TravelHost Magazine
5044 Bearcreek Road
Branson, MO 65615
417/334-5297

Sunny Day Guide
800 Seahawk Circle, Suite 106
Virginia Beach, VA 23452
www.sunnydayguide.com

Branson Take 1
Tri-Lakes Newspapers, Inc.
P.O. Box 1900
Branson, MO 65615
417/334-3161
(Published each Friday and included in the *Branson News,*
it contains coupons not found anywhere else)

Most of these magazines are five by eight inches or tabloid
size. Although the majority of them are available on a yearly
subscription basis, prices are sometimes high. You'll find these
magazines all over town after you arrive. Since they are helpful for advance planning, however, when you aren't able to get
them directly from their publishers, you might want to request
copies from the Branson Chamber of Commerce. Their ad-
dress and phone number are:

Branson/Lake Area Chamber of Commerce/CVB
P.O. Box 1897, 269 State Highway 248
Branson MO 65616
800/368-1441 or 417/334-4084
www.explorebranson.com

Discount coupons are especially important for families on
a tight vacation budget. They're great money stretchers when
you want to visit an attraction, eat at a restaurant, stay at a
hotel, or take a tour and can match up discount coupons with
those attractions or businesses.

Inflight magazines of airlines serving Springfield/Branson
Regional Airport often have ads containing freebie or discount
coupons, too. Coupons that give discounts on auto rentals can
be particularly helpful. Prior to your trip, obtain copies of inflight magazines of airlines that fly to Springfield/Branson
(flying with a particular airline isn't a requirement for use of
coupons found in their magazines).

Branson newspapers include the following (you might want to subscribe to them for a month prior to your trip, or for a longer period if you're considering a permanent move to the area):

Branson Daily News
120 North Commercial Street
Branson, MO 65616
417/334-3161

Taney County Times
220A West Pacific
Branson, MO 65616
417/334-2285

ACCOMMODATIONS

For ratings and basic information about various Branson lodging places, your best sources are the *AAA Arkansas, Kansas, Missouri, Oklahoma Tourbook,* available at American Automobile Association offices (free to members; $8.75 to nonmembers), and the *Mobil Travel Guide,* available at bookstores and at most public library reference desks.

It's possible to get additional information about accommodations by asking to see any of the hotel guides used by the travel agency you patronize. The *Star* ratings are especially good, as their evaluations of properties are extremely candid.

TRANSPORTATION

Drivers will be ahead of the game by obtaining a good map of Branson and studying it in advance. Having a general idea of which streets run in what directions can save time and tempers. Rand McNally's *Branson Map Guide* ($5.95, available at major bookstores) is one of the best and folds into a convenient 3- by nine-inch rectangle. The free maps obtainable from the chamber of commerce are excellent, too, and may be more up to date than those that are produced commercially.

DINING, SHOPPING, AND ATTRACTIONS

Discount coupons for many restaurants, a number of stores, and almost every attraction in Branson are available in free entertainment publications.

ACTIVITIES

Sending requests to the addresses listed below will provide you with information on fishing, camping, and other outdoor activities in the Branson area:

Missouri Fishing Regulations
Missouri Department of Conservation
P.O. Box 180
Jefferson City, MO 65102-0180
800/781-1989

Forest and Conservation Information
Department of Conservation
417/895-6880

State Park Information
Department of Natural Resources
417/334-4704

Table Rock Resident Office
U.S. Army Corps of Engineers
P.O. Box 1109
Branson, MO 65616
877/444-6777 or 417/334-4101
www.reserveusa.com

Among interesting books about the outdoors and other aspects of Missouri life that are available in Branson bookstores, as well as those nationwide, are *The Ozarks Outdoors: A Guide for Fishermen and Hunters* by Milton D. Rafferty, *Wild Edibles of Missouri* by Jan Phillips, and *Traditional Country Crafts* by Victoria Dalton.

SHOWS

The Branson Chamber of Commerce has several publications that tell you about Branson theaters and the shows presented in them, including prices. An especially useful Web site is wysiwyg://3http://www.bransonaccessamer.com/shows.html. The site lists all the Branson shows, allowing you to click on to those that have Web sites.

DAY TRIPS

To be sure you don't miss a thing on your day trips and excursions, get advance information on what to do and see:

Eureka Visitors Center
Highway 62 West, Eureka Springs, AR 72632
800/6-EUREKA

Springfield Convention & Visitors Bureau
Tourist Information Center
3315 East Battlefield Road
Springfield, MO 65804-4048

USEFUL WEB ADDRESSES

A great deal of information about Branson and other destinations is available on the Internet. Search engines Google and Yahoo are especially effective in providing multiple information sources. Among Web sites that should prove useful to you are the following:

General Information: www.bransonconnection.com

Accommodations: www.foreverresorts.com

Getting Around   www.bransongrayline.com

Attractions: www.big-cedar.com
www.bransonimax.com
www.stonehillwinery.com
www.tablerocklake.com
www.thousandhills.com

Activities:	www.americanparknetwork.com
	www.nps.gov
	www.xpressweb.com/parks
Day Trips:	www.silverdollarcity.com
	www.bransonusa.com
	www.eurekaspringschamber.com

One last suggestion: When you can't seem to find the information you're looking for, phone the reference desk at the Branson Library, 417/334-1418. The people there are almost sure to be able to answer your questions or to direct you to someone who can.

Index